China and the Pursui
Harmony in World Politics

Focusing on the role of harmony in Chinese international relations (IR) theory, this book seeks to illuminate Chinese understandings of world politics and foreign policy.

Taking a decolonial approach and rooted in China's cultural and epistemic terms, the title first describes three traditions of the concept of harmony in ancient Chinese thought and then analyses three strands of contemporary Chinese IR theory that draw upon this traditional thinking. Despite their similarities in advocating a radical deepening of China's relations with other countries and intense interdependence as essential for global peace and prosperity, these Chinese IR theories understand the concept of harmony in different ways and present different recommendations for achieving harmonious relations. Based on this framework of harmonious IR, Chinese social scientists also argue for new directions in Chinese foreign policy in a manner that is complementary with China's policymaking system. In the case-study section, the authors apply harmonious IR perspectives to the Belt and Road Initiative and demonstrate how a better understanding of Chinese IR theories can shed light on motivations behind Chinese foreign policy.

This work will be a valuable reference for scholars, students, policymakers, and general readers interested in Chinese politics, Chinese foreign policy, Chinese IR theory, and ancient Chinese philosophy.

Adam Grydehøj 葛陆海 is Chair Professor at South China University of Technology's Research Center for Indian Ocean Island Countries. His research concerns the intersection of culture, economy, politics, and space in island regions. He is Editor-in-Chief of *Island Studies Journal*.

Ping Su 苏娉 is Professor at South China University of Technology's Research Center for Indian Ocean Island Countries. She is an interdisciplinary scholar who researches island studies, urban migrants, the diasporic experience, international relations, and Caribbean literature.

China Perspectives

The *China Perspectives* series focuses on translating and publishing works by leading Chinese scholars, writing about both global topics and China-related themes. It covers Humanities & Social Sciences, Education, Media and Psychology, as well as many interdisciplinary themes.

This is the first time any of these books have been published in English for international readers. The series aims to put forward a Chinese perspective, give insights into cutting-edge academic thinking in China, and inspire researchers globally.

To submit proposals, please contact the Taylor & Francis Publisher for the China Publishing Programme, Lian Sun (Lian.Sun@informa.com)

Recent titles in politics partly include

The Routledge Handbook of Chinese Citizenship
Edited by Zhonghua Guo

The Transformation of American Political Culture and the Impact on Foreign Strategy
PAN Yaling

China and Africa in Global Context
Encounters, Policy, Cooperation and Migration
LI Anshan

China and the Pursuit of Harmony in World Politics
Understanding Chinese International Relations Theory
Adam Grydehøj and Ping Su

For more information, please visit www.routledge.com/China-Perspectives/book-series/CPH

China and the Pursuit of Harmony in World Politics

Understanding Chinese International Relations Theory

Adam Grydehøj and Ping Su

Routledge
Taylor & Francis Group

LONDON AND NEW YORK

First published 2022
by Routledge
2 Park Square, Milton Park, Abingdon, Oxon OX14 4RN

and by Routledge
605 Third Avenue, New York, NY 10158

Routledge is an imprint of the Taylor & Francis Group, an informa business

British Library Cataloguing-in-Publication Data
A catalogue record for this book is available from the British Library

Library of Congress Cataloging-in-Publication Data
Names: Grydehøj, Adam, author. | Su, Ping, 1983– author.
Title: China and the pursuit of harmony in world politics :
   understanding Chinese international relations theory /
   Adam Grydehøj and Ping Su.
Description: London ; New York, NY : Routledge, Taylor &
   Francis Group, 2022. | Series: China perspectives. Politics |
   Includes bibliographical references and index.
Identifiers: LCCN 2021039248 (print) | LCCN 2021039249 (ebook)
Subjects: LCSH: China—Foreign relations. | China—Politics and
   government.
Classification: LCC DS740.4 .G79 2022 (print) | LCC DS740.4 (ebook) |
   DDC 327.51—dc23/eng/20211019
LC record available at https://lccn.loc.gov/2021039248
LC ebook record available at https://lccn.loc.gov/2021039249

ISBN: 978-1-032-19466-0 (hbk)
ISBN: 978-1-032-19563-6 (pbk)
ISBN: 978-1-003-25979-4 (ebk)

DOI: 10.4324/9781003259794

Typeset in Times New Roman
by Apex CoVantage, LLC

Contents

Figures

1 Introduction

The world is everything

The great Chinese international relations (IR) theorist Qin Yaqing begins his book on world politics with a metaphor: the social scientist is like a person standing on a mountain, only able to see from their own perspective, forever unable to view the mountain in its entirety.[1]

We are part of the world, and the world is everything. There is no inside or outside. So we use metaphors to make reality more manageable.

The metaphors we choose are significant. They are a result of how we see the world, and they affect how we act in the world. If your metaphor for the world is a garden, then perhaps you might think of planting trees. If your metaphor is a stormy sea,[2] you might seek safe harbour. If your metaphor is a beehive, you might attempt to emulate bees' industriousness, foresight, artistry, craft, fraternal selflessness, or adherence to hierarchical structures, all depending on what it was that attracted you to bees in the first place.[3]

This book is about theory. More specifically, it is about IR theories, which aim to help us understand world politics. More specifically still, it is about how IR theories that originate in different parts of the world may (or may not) produce different visions of the world.

To assist us in understanding this rather abstract topic, we too use a metaphor. Our metaphor illustrates the relationship between theorists, the world of theory, and the world itself.

Ours is a metaphor of gardens.

A metaphor of gardens

You are standing in a classical garden somewhere in China, looking out over a lake. Perhaps you are in Hangzhou, at West Lake. Or at the Summer Palace, in Beijing, Xuanwu Lake, in Nanjing, or Luhu Lake, in Guangzhou. The specific garden matters; all these gardens are different. But for the purpose of our metaphor, any of these gardens will do.

DOI: 10.4324/9781003259794-1

We will call it a 'Chinese garden'.

You are standing in a Chinese garden, looking out over a lake. If it is a sunny day, the surface of the lake reflects the trees along the shore and the green mountains beyond. Or perhaps mist rises from the lake, obscuring trees and mountains, merging land, water, and sky. A sprinkling of islands. A pagoda would be appropriate. Somewhere on the opposite shore, a vertical bridge between heaven and lake.

These are visions of nature in harmony. But the Chinese garden is not 'natural' in the sense in which the term is usually understood in the West. The mountains have been landscaped, possibly for agricultural, religious, or aesthetic purposes. The trees by the shore have been planted and maintained. The pagoda looks as though it has always been there, but it too has been built and rebuilt over the centuries. The lake is artificial, comprehensively transformed and sculpted from its ancient original form, now lost to our imperfect knowledge. The garden as a whole is the work of a succession of individual people—we may call them 'landscape architects'—who envisioned perfect forms for the garden and overlaid these upon those which came before, in ages past.

But it is not only, or even mostly, landscape architects who have produced the garden. There have also been countless numbers of gardeners, who have created and maintained the garden out of land, water, and sky, sometimes cleaving closely to the vision of this or that landscape architect but always, inevitably, adding something of themselves to the work. And there have been rulers, merchants, farmers, monks, poets, tourists, tour guides, and so many more whose ideas about the garden have conditioned landscape architects' visions of what could be possible and how, in collaboration with others, their landscape vision could be put into practice.

The garden is not the world. (Who could mistake a mere garden for the whole world?) The garden is but an intervention in our way of understanding the world. The garden is a theory, and the landscape architect is one of its many theorists. The landscape architect must envision a garden that strikes a balance between creating an ideal world and working within the real world. This balance must be struck, for a garden that too plainly diverges from the reality of the world is a garden that cannot inspire others to act in a certain manner in the world.

Within traditional Chinese culture, harmony is the ideal state of the world. This is encapsulated in the ancient concept of *tian ren he yi* (天人合一), literally 'unity of heaven and humankind'. When translated into English, *tian* (天) often becomes 'nature', rather than 'heaven'. This elision is misleading: from a Western perspective, 'unity of *nature* and humankind' suggests that humans are part of and inseparable from nature. People must understand they are part of a natural system. This is an argument against

Figure 1.1 A Chinese garden.

Source: Lin Guangyu, 2021

anthropocentrism: who do humans think they are, to believe they can control nature?

From a traditional Chinese perspective, 'unity of *heaven* and humankind' asserts that humans carry out the will of heaven. Through virtuous behaviour, humans contribute to the harmonious ordering of the world, in line with heavenly precepts. Everyone, whether ruler or peasant, landscape architect or gardener, embodies heaven, though differences in social status and station mean that this (ideally) comes to expression in different ways for different people. In this worldview, humans are not merely part of the world; virtuous human action is essential to the proper ordering of the world.

This, at least, is one vision of Chinese culture and tradition. Its existence does not exclude the existence of others.

We return to the Chinese garden, with its lake, trees, islands, pagoda, mountains, sky. Humans have created the garden to reinforce the world's pre-existing or ideal harmony. An understanding of the world as flowing toward harmony encouraged a landscape architecture and gardening practice conducive to deepening harmonious thought.

But let us say you are standing in a different garden, in a formal garden somewhere in Europe. Perhaps at Versailles, outside Paris, Villa di Castello, in Florence, or Frederiksborg Castle, in Hillerød. We will call it a 'European garden'. There are ponds. There are plants, a palace, and, indeed, sky. The garden juxtaposes these various elements: in straight lines, in perfect curves, in strict spatial divisions, ruled by geometry.[4] Although both the Chinese garden and the European garden seek to order nature, their ambitions and effects diverge. Whereas the Chinese garden creates harmony by merging elements and bringing them into reflection and interaction, the European garden creates peace by balancing distinct features alongside, within, and atop one another, without compromising their autonomy.

Both kinds of gardens are the result of immense and continual human labour, but the Chinese garden pursues the illusion of effortlessness, of happy circumstance, of being a product of natural processes. In contrast, the European garden is forthright about its origins in processes of control. It foregrounds power and effort. A worldview that sees power as emanating from central points encourages a landscape architecture practice that heightens attentiveness to the sources of this power and the centrality of control. These two opposing impulses make it difficult to gain an understanding of gardens in general: gardening practice trembles within "a polarity, which has on the one side nature and on the other the human ego."[5]

We must not be essentialist. There are informal gardens in Europe, including whole traditions of landscape architecture emphasising ambiguous relations between elements.[6] There are also formal gardens in China. Even so culturally significant a site as the Forbidden City, in Beijing, has been constructed in an architecture redolent of centralised power. And while classical Chinese gardens reflected wider Chinese thought, the cosmologies within this thought changed over time and across space, producing gardens attuned in different ways to Shamanistic, Taoist, Confucian, and Buddhist traditions.[7] Furthermore, classic Chinese gardens, though envisioned as microcosms, specifically matched the microcosmic imaginations of the social elite, of scholars and officials.[8] What does it say about the connection between gardens and culture that Chinese tradition could simultaneously inspire so fluid and decentralised a garden as the one in which we have chosen to stand and so fixed and centralised a garden as the Forbidden City? Is it even possible to understand gardens in general if we cannot do so simply by studying particular, individual gardens?

So let us be clear. Our Chinese garden is not the only garden in China, and it certainly is not 'China'. It is just a garden. But it is this particular garden that *we* have chosen as the best site for contemplating the nature of gardens. After all, everyone must stand somewhere. Every study is conditioned by its positioning. No study, however abstract its subject, exists without context.

This metaphor of gardens expresses the premise of the present book. Neither the Chinese nor the European garden is inherently right or wrong, better or worse than the other, yet the two types rely upon different epistemologies or ways of thinking. From the perspective of someone immersed in the deceptive naturalism of Hangzhou's West Lake, the meticulous symmetry and effortful artifice of the Gardens of Versailles would be far from harmonious—and vice versa.

The two gardens represent different understandings of gardens and thus of the world as a whole. The way we see the world changes how we act in the world: the European landscape architect has no desire to envision a Chinese garden. Theorists who perceive the world in different ways will create different theories to reflect and improve practices in the world.

About this book

This book concerns the role of 'harmony' in present-day IR theory in China and how harmony-oriented IR theories influence and are influenced by Chinese foreign policy.

The Chinese IR theorists who we consider in this book are not, generally speaking, particularly interested in structuring their work and expressing their arguments in ways that resemble major schools of mainstream IR scholarship. This has, in fact, been part of the reason why Chinese IR theory has not always been recognised or acknowledged as theory.[9] It would thus be counterproductive to insist upon strict definitions of what 'theory' means within mainstream IR. From the perspectives of the Chinese IR discipline, we might define IR theory as explanations of existing or ideal interactions between polities (states, territories, nations, ethnic groups, and other communities). In order to easily differentiate IR practice from IR as a scholarly discipline, we use the term 'foreign policy' to refer to a polity's approach to interacting with other polities, and we use the term 'world politics' to refer to the totality of interactions among polities.

Harmony (和谐 *hexie*) is often said to be a key concept in Chinese culture, yet its role in the history of Chinese civilisation is both complex and contested.[10] As we shall see, harmonious relations are key both as a method and as a goal of Chinese IR theory. Although harmony has been recognised as significant for the Chinese government's rhetorical strategy,[11] there has been little attempt to compare the uses of harmony in Chinese IR theories and to apply these to world politics and foreign policy practice. This is despite the fact that Chinese IR scholarship exists in complex interaction with Chinese policymaking and wider ideas of what it means to be Chinese in the world.

Such comparative study of harmony in Chinese IR theory is important, in part because there has never been a consensus understanding of harmony itself in China. As is perhaps fitting for a concept that is said to be the "cardinal cultural value in Chinese society,"[12] the meaning of harmony has always been flexible and ambiguous. Harmonious world politics can mean many different things, and harmony finds idiosyncratic expression in various Chinese IR theories. Harmony can be a statement of intent, a dream of an ideal world, a description of the world in its natural state, a tool for resolving or averting conflict with the state, a lever for enhancing influence on the realm of practice—or, most often, something in between. When deployed by the state, discourses of harmony can be an appeal for peaceful relations of equality, a buttress for existing positions of authority, a radical decentring mechanism, or a powerful centring gesture. To say that harmony is one thing is not to say that it cannot be something else. To say that harmony is ambiguous or idealistic is not to say that it has no influence on the world.

Taken as a whole, this book is an argument for the importance of understanding theory on its own, culturally contingent terms. By extension, it is an argument for attentiveness to cultural or epistemic difference when analysing processes in world politics.

In Chapter 2, we discuss the relationships between culture, theory, and methods. We begin by discussing the need to consider Chinese perspectives before situating our own work within decolonial scholarship and offering a brief review of our methods. In Chapter 3, we present a short overview of the concept of harmony in ancient and imperial China, emphasising the diversity of meanings held by harmony in different intellectual traditions and at different periods. In Chapter 4, we sequentially describe and analyse three prominent Chinese IR theories that involve a focus on harmony:

tianxia (天下) theory, *guanxi* (关系) theory, and *gongsheng* (共生) theory. In Chapter 5, we analyse the connections between the realms of research and policymaking in China. We consider how the three selected theories utilise traditional Chinese concepts as a means of critiquing present-day foreign policy practice in a language that is complementary with China's policymaking environment. We then consider the criticism that Chinese IR theory is ethnonationalist and exceptionalist, arguing both that this criticism involves a misunderstanding of the ways in which the theories have been designed and that the criticism sometimes reveals a blindness to its own Western epistemic positioning. In Chapter 6, we apply the three selected Chinese IR theories to foreign policy practice by seeking to understand discourses of harmony within the Chinese state's Belt and Road Initiative. We do so in part by presenting examples of how the theories are used in the wider Chinese social science scholarship. We conclude and summarise the main findings of the book in Chapter 7.

Notes

1 Qin 2018, ix.
2 Constable 2008.
3 Ramírez 2000.
4 Cheng et al. 2019.
5 Naydler 2021, 9.
6 Hansen 2018.
7 Tceluiko 2019.
8 Stuart 1990.
9 Acharya & Buzan 2007.
10 Wang 2010; Wei & Li 2013.
11 Zheng & Tok 2007; Alvaro 2013; Nordin 2016.
12 Wei & Li 2013, 60.

References

Acharya A, & Buzan B (2007). Why is there no non-Western international relations theory? An introduction. *International Relations of the Asia-Pacific, 7*(3), 287–312.

Alvaro JJ (2013). Political discourse in China's English language press. *World Englishes, 32*(2), 147–168.

Cheng G, Yu Y, He T, Lin C, & Luo L (2019). A brief analysis of the successful experience of French classical gardens for the construction of Chinese gardens. *Asian Agricultural Research, 11*(11), 28–30.

Constable G (2008). Metaphors for religious life in the Middle Ages. *Revue Mabillon, 19*, 231–242.

Hansen MF (2018). *The art of transformation: Grotesques in sixteenth-century Italy*. Edizioni Quasar.

Naydler J (2021). *Gardening as a sacred art: Towards the redemption of our relationship with nature*. Temple Lodge.

Nordin AH (2016). *China's international relations and harmonious world: Time, space and multiplicity in world politics*. Routledge.

Qin Y (2018). *A relational theory of world politics*. Cambridge University Press.

Ramírez JA (2000). *The beehive metaphor: From Gaudí to Le Corbusier*. Reaktion.

Stuart J (1990). Ming dynasty gardens reconstructed in words and images. *The Journal of Garden History, 10*(3), 162–172.

Tceluiko DS (2019). Influence of Shamanism, Taoism, Buddhism and Confucianism on development of traditional Chinese gardens. *IOP Conference Series: Materials Science and Engineering, 687*(5), 55041.

Wang YK (2010). *Harmony and war: Confucian culture and Chinese power politics*. Columbia University Press.

Wei X, & Li Q (2013). The Confucian value of harmony and its influence on Chinese social interaction. *Cross-Cultural Communication, 9*(1), 60–66.

Zheng Y, & Tok SK (2007). Harmonious society and harmonious world: China's policy discourse under Hu Jintao. *Briefing Series, 26*, 1–12.

2   Culture, theory, and methods

The need to consider Chinese perspectives

In China, in the West, and elsewhere in the world, in the mass media, in scholarly literature, and in government pronouncements, there is agreement: China is a 'rising power'.[1]

Despite a consensus that China is 'going places', there is a lack of agreement as to where it is headed. Whereas some perceive China's rise as endangering the natural environment, risking military conflict, and producing poverty and exploitation, others see it as an opportunity for engaging in fairer, more sustainable, or simply different developmental pathways. As in our metaphor of gardens, it may not be so simple as to say that one position is right and the other is wrong. China's disruptive influence on the international order may simultaneously be threatening for some polities and advantageous for others. Current great powers may have good reason to fear their privileged status is at risk, while nations that have experienced colonialism or have otherwise been poorly served by world politics may welcome alternatives.[2]

The very idea of zero-sum competition between great powers is a rational approach to world politics only if one ignores the perspectives of other international actors. Even the smallest of polities see themselves as active participants in global political and economic processes, rather than as mere sites of contention or playthings manipulated by great powers.[3] The outlooks and perspectives of different polities do not arise independently of one another: all knowledge is co-produced, all geographies are created through relational processes, and even efforts to engage in decolonial theory may struggle to escape "binary thinking and metropolitan orientations."[4]

What is true for small countries is true for China: perspective matters. Although China is now indisputably a powerful economic, cultural, and political force, China is not yet a major force in the world of ideas. For all the discussion among scholars, policymakers, and media commentators in

DOI: 10.4324/9781003259794-2

the West concerning China's role in world politics and the Chinese government's foreign policy ambitions, there is relatively little interest in understanding how their Chinese peers perceive world politics. As a result, policy and strategy pronouncements by the Chinese government tend to be interpreted within Western theoretical frameworks.

Western IR theories are legitimate on their own terms. There is nothing wrong with applying Western theories to Chinese topics. To return to our metaphor of gardens, a European landscape architect should not be expected to set aside their worldview when assessing the aesthetic and social qualities of Chinese classical gardens. Awareness that other people value other things does not force someone to value all things equally, regardless of personal preference. We might, however, expect our European landscape architect to understand the Chinese garden as something other than just a failed European garden. In fact, we might expect that, if the European landscape architect inspects the Chinese garden—with its knobbly rockeries, subtle transitions between elements, and disdain for symmetry—they will recognise a different logic at work than that which guides their own theories of how gardening ought to be practiced.

In scholarship more generally, there is a growing understanding that theory is culturally contingent. This is especially evident in decolonial scholarship, as discussed in the next section. Social actors may have divergent priorities and perceive reality in different ways. Studies concerning a particular people or place are increasingly expected to engage with scholarship arising from the context in question, regardless of the researchers' own nationalities, ethnicities, or places of employment. This is sometimes intended as a corrective to existing power imbalances. It also involves recognition that, when seeking to understand a society, it helps to listen to those within it. Discussing Indigenous studies, Todd argues that Indigenous thinkers should be cited "directly, unambiguously and generously. As thinkers in their own right, not just disembodied representatives of an amorphous Indigeneity that serves European intellectual or political purposes," and researchers of Indigenous communities should avoid simply "filtering ideas through white intermediaries."[5] The same is true for studies of any frequently 'othered' community.

Only a small minority of Western studies of Chinese foreign policy and China's role in world politics engage at all with the work of Chinese researchers. Writing in the mid-2000s, Amitav Acharya and Barry Buzan note that, despite its global subject matter, "almost all [IR theory] is produced by and for the West, and rests on an assumption that Western history is world history," running the risk of Western IR being "seen as the particular, parochial, and Eurocentric, self-interestedly pretending to be universal."[6]

Western IR's lack of engagement with Chinese IR theory partially comes down to the inaccessibility of key scholarly texts for those who do not read

Chinese, though some of the most prominent Chinese IR theorists have published substantial works in English.[7] More broadly, studies of Chinese policy are often grounded in a conception of China as a monolithic, unitary state actor. There is thus a tendency to regard Chinese scholars as representatives of a national whole, rather than to accord them the status of individual researchers, albeit individual researchers engaged in thinking through what it means to be part of an envisioned national collective. This is not primarily a matter of anti-Chinese sentiment; it instead involves a lack of understanding of why a good-faith actor might reasonably make particular decisions. Insufficient knowledge of other cultural contexts causes the motivations behind actions in world politics to be understood from a Western perspective, even when the actors themselves are approaching matters from a different perspective. As a result, actors are deemed to be either unreasonable or not acting in good faith.

There is today a thriving Chinese IR research community, which has produced approaches to studying world politics that are perceived in China as specifically 'Chinese'. Chinese IR research simultaneously and variously works to justify, highlight shortcomings of, and inspire Chinese foreign policy. There are nevertheless numerous gaps in the English-language literature concerning Chinese IR research, both in describing Chinese IR theories and in analysing how they relate to one another, to Chinese foreign policy, and to wider Chinese society. Even within China, commonalities between various theoretical approaches often go unanalysed. For example, this book's focus on the concept of harmony in Chinese IR theories has thus far not been comparatively discussed in either English or Chinese-language publications, with a few partial exceptions,[8] even though each of the theories brings harmony to the forefront of their arguments.

We follow Emilian Kavalski in asserting the possibility of engaging with theory in a "culturally-attuned" manner, without needing to "constantly qualify, bracket, and signpost . . . engagement with non-Western ideas."[9] This book is a study of—rather than a defence or condemnation of—Chinese IR theory and foreign policy rhetoric. We do not seek to ascertain the extent to which the promise of foreign policy rhetoric is fulfilled in foreign policy practice. This is in part because world political processes always involve numerous actors and are not determined by any one polity alone. It is also in part because we believe it valuable to consider the ways in which core concepts such as harmony operate within Chinese society; debate over whether this or that policy is truly conducive to harmony in world politics in practice is not always conducive to such inquiry, especially given that, as we argue here, harmony itself is being constantly negotiated and reassessed as a concept.

Similarly, we do not seek to understand Chinese IR theory through analogy with theories from elsewhere: comparing Chinese and non-Chinese theories is an important task, but it first presumes a strong understanding of the variety and shared characteristics within Chinese theory. When we do engage in cross-cultural comparison, such as with our metaphor of gardens, it is from a perspective linked specifically to the Chinese IR community, making no claims to objective universalism. This is, indeed, in keeping with strands of harmony-oriented IR theory, which foreground rootedness in a particular relational position.[10] Every study stands somewhere and sees the world from some perspective.

Epistemic difference and decolonial theory

Why does it matter that every study stands somewhere? There is a tension at the heart of many Chinese IR theories. Although they seek to compete, in a sense, with Western IR theories, they do not necessarily have the same premises as Western IR theories. Of the Chinese approaches considered in this book, only one (*tianxia* theory) insists on its own universality. The others (*guanxi* and *gongsheng* theory) envision a distinctively Chinese IR. They do not argue that Western approaches are incapable of producing a correct understanding of world politics; they simply argue that Chinese approaches are also capable of this and that taking a Chinese approach may be advantageous in some circumstances. All three theories advance claims of Chinese epistemic difference, of special Chinese ways of knowing the world.

Epistemologies develop within communities. Discussing the Kwara'ae cultural group in Malaita, Solomon Islands, David Welchman Gegeo and Karen Anne Watson-Gegeo define 'Indigenous epistemology' as

> a cultural group's ways of thinking and of creating, reformulating, and theorizing about knowledge via traditional discourses and media of communication, anchoring the truth of the discourse in culture. As a concept, indigenous epistemology focuses on the process through which knowledge is constructed and validated by a cultural group, and the role of that process in shaping thinking and behavior. It assumes all epistemological systems to be socially constructed and (in)formed through sociopolitical, economic, and historical context and processes. It also recognizes that culture is variable, an ongoing conversation embodying conflict and change.[11]

Epistemologies are always changing, never static. Even when, as in Kwara'ae and particular Chinese communities, discussions of epistemology often revolve around tradition and ancient precedent, it is always tradition and ancient precedent as seen through today's eyes. Epistemologies are not monolithic but are instead constructed out of social contestation. For example, the prevalence of harmony in both official and unofficial discourses today has prompted some Chinese scholars to critically assess how the concept is implicated in certain problematic logics.[12] Such contention is central to the how epistemologies develop over time.

The preceding definition of epistemology rightly suggests that the world is full of distinctive epistemologies, yet discussions of epistemic difference (even in the present book) often slide into the easy framework of a West/non-West binary. Within this binary, 'the West' is one thing, and 'the non-West' is another. This is no coincidence. The 'non-West' is itself a product of coloniality, a category that piles together all that has been excluded from the West's sense of self. In the words of decolonial scholar Walter Mignolo:

> The enduring enchantment of binary oppositions seems to be related to the enduring image of a European civilization and of European history told from the perspective of Europe itself. Europe is not only the center (that is, the center of space and the point of arrival in time) but also has the epistemic privilege of being the center of enunciation.[13]

Western thought has the privilege of seeing itself as a universal standard and of interpreting the world in its own image. This privilege is unavailable to Chinese thought, which has developed in response to Western theoretical dominance. Gegeo and Watson-Gegeo write, "All knowledge is subjective knowledge in Kwara'ae: there can be no detachment of the knower from the known as in mainstream Anglo-European epistemology."[14] This can be said of most epistemologies that lack the privilege of taking their own universality for granted.

Such a position is, however, challenging for mainstream (Western) scholarship, which denies the situatedness of its own knowledge, insists upon the potential for theory that is not rooted in culture, and seeks to freeze non-Western ways of knowing within temporally and spatially specific boundaries.[15] Some scholars criticise claims of epistemic difference for essentialising and entrenching faulty Western/non-Western binaries. For example, Christopher Murray argues:

> Adding ethnicised or culturalist representations of non-Western traits will never deliver a global or post-imperial IR. Adding ethnic and cultural variations on IR concepts such as sovereignty, agency, or cosmopolitanism contributes to a world divided by imperial categories, and props up the subordinate power claims of local universalisms. . . . Thus epistemic difference should not be seen simply as a reflection of an externally existing reality, but as a process of representation which is power laden and dialectical.[16]

Because Murray's argument is based on close readings of and praise for important Black liberationist writers of the past (W.E.B. Du Bois and Frantz Fanon), it is ostensibly supportive of anti-imperial movements. Yet Murray's use of historical thinkers to delegitimise the work of today's decolonial and anti-imperial thinkers (including numerous researchers connected with Chinese IR) suggests otherwise.

Writing in the context of North American settler colonialism, Eve Tuck and K. Wayne Yang conceptualise 'settler moves to innocence', which they define as "strategies or positionings that attempt to relieve the settler of feelings of guilt or responsibility without giving up land or power or privilege, without having to change much at all."[17] For Elena Ruíz, mainstream scholarship tends to pathologise decolonial thought and make it doubt itself, "a form of epistemic territorial expansion that empowers members of dominant communities to claim epistemic space as their own, and only their own," even as they "genuinely think they are doing good."[18] Ruíz's concerns apply to all circumstances in which the West takes itself as standard, and she notes that "marginalized knowledge-creators must [prove] the legitimacy of our ideas by demonstrating that they are at the very least adjacent to and comprehensible within recognizable settler epistemic frameworks."[19] This need to prove legitimacy is especially pernicious as it makes self-erasure a condition for acceptance. The inability of one epistemology or power system to conceive of a thing does not negate this thing's existence. Yet cultures end up being translated back to themselves in a rupture between land, discourse, language, and personhood.[20]

As we shall see, Chinese IR theories are both developing in reaction to Western epistemic dominance and being subject to Western denials of epistemic difference. Trenchant critics of Chinese IR argue, from diverse political philosophical starting points, that Chinese IR theory *should not* exist because the struggle against imperialism necessitates the equality of all peoples.[21] It is furthermore often implied that because the hard work of formal decolonisation has already ended and equality has been achieved, it is now time to move on to other, more pressing concerns.

However, until the terms of this purported equality cease to be precisely those terms developed in Western thought, such arguments will remain efforts to change the subject, to defend Western epistemic privilege, to delegitimise decolonial approaches at their points of origin. As Kathryn Yusoff suggests in her critique of Anthropocene scholarship, it is highly convenient for the West to make common cause with the non-West—on the condition that the non-West forgets about the systemic injustices and racialised catastrophes that continue to privilege Western definitions and worldviews.[22]

Universalism grounded in Western definitions of equality is not the answer. Indeed, Mignolo sees the unequal language of universalism as productive of coloniality:

[Western] knowledge-construction made it possible to eliminate or marginalize what did not fit into those principles that aspired to build a totality in which everybody would be included, but not everybody would also have the right to include. Inclusion is a one-way street and not a reciprocal right. In a world governed by the colonial matrix of power, he who includes and she who is welcomed to be included stand in codified power relations. The locus of enunciation from which inclusion is established is always a locus holding the control of knowledge and the power of decision.[23]

In other words, it is not enough for the Western IR community to proclaim that it welcomes the inclusion of scholars from China and other places outside the West. It is absurd to confuse 1) the potential for inclusion within Western frameworks with 2) the ability to construct one's own frameworks. A universalism that grants everyone personhood on Western terms is no replacement for the opportunity to set one's own terms.[24]

The present book takes a decolonial stand against the idea that theory can be separated from epistemology, that knowledge can exist without a specific knower. This requires not just disputing the universality of Western thought but also disputing the generalisability of non-Western thought.[25] The Chinese IR theories we consider in this book identify themselves as simultaneously Chinese *and* non-Western. Chinese epistemology, so much as such a thing may exist, is not interchangeable with other non-Western epistemologies. When Chinese scholars theorise on a Chinese epistemic basis, it is not because 'China' is designed to supplant 'the West' in a binary struggle. Only the West is capable of imagining itself as the world standard. Chinese scholars theorise on a Chinese epistemic basis because this is, quite simply, how they know their work. They are entitled to work their own ground, without the necessity of first conquering someone else's theoretical domain.

We thus insist upon the right of a community to know its own things, in its own ways. 'Epistemology' is, as Manulani Aluli-Meyer notes, a compromising term: it is awkward to root one's decolonial argument in the philosophical tradition of ancient Greece.[26] When we conceive of epistemology in this book, it is in the sense that many of the Chinese IR theorists under discussion assert the existence of a distinctive Chinese way of thinking and knowing. These theorists do indeed seem to be engaging in a different kind of knowledge production than is common in mainstream IR: the theories we consider here all involve the creation of world politics knowledge through harmonious practice. There is a kind of circular causation and ambiguity of cause and effect. In addition, the concept of harmony itself, which we find to be so central to some Chinese IR theories, plays little role in Western IR and, as we shall see, does not appear to be a point of foreign policy focus in the West. Whatever the strengths and weaknesses of the Chinese IR theories considered here, they follow different methods and priorities than are common in mainstream IR—regardless of whether one accepts their claims of seeking to improve world politics or whether one believes the theories have propagandistic or ethnonationalist intent.

We pass no judgement on whether these theorists' analyses of Chinese epistemology are correct or incorrect. Certainly, there are other scholars who argue that Chinese epistemology is multiple (rather than unitary)[27] or that it is best pursued in combination with alternative ways of knowing.[28] We might furthermore note that the theorists whose views we consider here do not represent a cross-section of Chinese society: they are instead overwhelmingly employed at universities and overwhelmingly men. Yet knowledge is by definition known by someone, in some place. Epistemology is always produced through contestation and discussion.

In asserting the legitimacy of arguments based on epistemic difference, we also wish to draw attention to the subtle epistemic violence underlying so much of the mainstream scholarly literature, which focuses more on disputing the notion of 'Chinese IR' or guarding the gates of the IR discipline than on getting to grips with individual Chinese IR theories.

Studying harmony in Chinese IR theory

This book developed out of a separate research project concerning how island communities with colonial histories (Guåhan/Guam, Jamaica, Kalaallit Nunaat/Greenland, and Okinawa) perceive Western warnings about a 'China threat'. This work of decolonial political geography found that Western political discourse regarding China often itself seemed trapped in a neocolonial mindset.[29] In the course of that research, we noted a common thread in Western responses to Chinese international activity, namely the idea that China was not acting in good faith and that its claims of benignity could not be believed.

This begged the question of which Chinese claims were being interpreted in this manner. What emerged was a Western distrust of the discourse of harmony, which (as we shall see) is indeed ubiquitous in Chinese foreign policy discussions and official pronouncements. Because the Western states in question were concerned with maintaining geopolitical dominance in certain territories and regions, a discourse of harmony that appealed to ideals of cooperation and equality were perceived as unbelievable. There seemed to be, at the very least, a discursive and perhaps even an epistemic divide.

This led us to enquire into what Chinese IR scholars were themselves saying about harmony. To achieve this, in June 2020, we undertook a non-systematic review of major trends in recent Chinese IR research. Although we considered English-language sources by Chinese authors where available, we relied on the larger body of Chinese-language literature. All translations of Chinese-language sources are our own. The relatively small size of the field of Chinese IR scholarship[30] allowed us to detect the most significant literature by following citation chains. We began our sampling by searching CNKI's China Academic Journals Full-Text Database for two keywords: 和谐 (*hexie* harmony) and 国际关系 (*guojiguanxi* international relations). We subsequently searched for 国际关系 in tandem with 和谐世界 (*hexie shijie* harmonious world) or 人类命运共同体 (*renlei mingyun gongtongti* community of common destiny, also known as community of shared future). 和谐 is a traditional Chinese concept, 国际关系 is a translation of the English-language term 'international relations', and 和谐世界 and 人类命运共同体 have been overarching Chinese policy frameworks in the first decades of the 21st century. We then undertook targeted Google Scholar searches for English-language literature. We identified four strands of theory (*tianxia, guanxi, gongsheng,* and *daoyi*) as particularly influential in today's Chinese IR community, and we further identified the first three of these as strongly linked with the concept of harmony. Having made this identification, we proceeded with more narrowly targeted research into scholarly literature concerning or utilising these theories.

The theories considered here are not the only influential IR theories in China, and they are not necessarily any more 'Chinese' than other theories. A major limitation to our study is that its purposeful sampling could be assumed to result in an overrepresentation of literature utilising harmony. The present study thus should not be read as an overview of or introduction to Chinese IR theory but should be understood as an exploration of how a particular concept and its associated worldviews, rooted in a particular epistemology, play out in theory-making and in theory's relationship with wider society.

We focus on Chinese researchers not to devalue the work of other researchers but in recognition that discussions *about* China in international scholarship have until now far exceeded articles *from* China. Because research traditions are tied to culture and circumstance, we focus on Chinese scholars based in the Chinese mainland, largely excluding the scholarship being produced in Macao SAR, Hong Kong SAR, and Taiwan. These polities are all shared inheritors of ancient Chinese intellectual traditions, but epistemology is not static and is more than just the work of ancient thinkers. The polities each possess distinctive political and scholarly histories that would complicate our own project's coherence and usefulness.

Notes

1 Kim 2016, 59; Zhang 2015.
2 Smith & Wesley-Smith 2021; Rodd 2020; Szadziewski 2020.
3 Davis, Munger, & Legacy 2020; Korson, Poaouteta, & Prinsen 2020; Grydehøj 2020.

4 Grydehøj et al. 2021; see also Nadarajah & Grydehøj 2016; Xie, Zhu, & Grydehøj 2020.
5 Todd 2016, 7.
6 Acharya & Buzan 2007, 288, 300.
7 Zhao 2009; Qin 2018; Yan 2013, 2019.
8 Hagström & Nordin, 2020; Kavalski, 2018.
9 Kavalski 2018, 235.
10 Xie, Zhu, & Grydehøj 2020.
11 Gegeo & Watson-Gegeo 2001, 58.
12 Guo 2006; Zhou 2007; Wang 2006.
13 Mignolo 2002, 908.
14 Gegeo & Watson-Gegeo 2001, 62.
15 Gegeo 2001.
16 Murray 2020, 420–421.
17 Tuck & Yang 2012, 10.
18 Ruíz 2020, 703.
19 Ruíz 2020, 699.
20 Nadarajah 2021.
21 See, e.g., Murray 2020; Callahan 2008.
22 Yusoff 2018.
23 Mignolo 2011, xv.
24 Guerin 2021.
25 Chandler & Reid 2020.
26 Meyer 2001.
27 Xu 2015.
28 Ling 2017.
29 Grydehøj et al. 2021.
30 Guo 2017, 22.

References

Acharya A, & Buzan B (2007). Why is there no non-Western international relations theory? An introduction. *International Relations of the Asia-Pacific*, 7(3), 287–312.

Callahan WA (2008). Chinese visions of world order: Post-hegemonic or a new hegemony? *International Studies Review*, 10(4), 749–761.

Chandler D, & Reid J (2020). Becoming Indigenous: The "speculative turn" in anthropology and the (re) colonisation of indigeneity. *Postcolonial Studies*, 23(4), 485–504.

Davis S, Munger LA, & Legacy HJ (2020). Someone else's chain, someone else's road: US military strategy, China's Belt and Road Initiative, and island agency in the Pacific. *Island Studies Journal*, 15(2), 13–36.

Gegeo DW (2001). Cultural rupture and indigeneity: The challenge of (re)visioning "place" in the Pacific. *The Contemporary Pacific*, 13(2), 491–507.

Gegeo DW, & Watson-Gegeo KA (2001). "How we know": Kwara'ae rural villagers doing indigenous epistemology. *The Contemporary Pacific*, 13(1), 55–88.

Grydehøj A (2020). Unravelling economic dependence and independence in relation to island sovereignty: The case of Kalaallit Nunaat (Greenland). *Island Studies Journal*, 15(1), 89–112.

Grydehøj A, Bevacqua ML, Chibana M, Nadarajah Y, Simonsen A, Su P, Wright R, & Davis S (2021). Practicing decolonial political geography: Island perspectives on neocolonialism and the China threat discourse. *Political Geography*, *85*, 102330.

Guerin A (2021). Shared routes of mammalian kinship: Race and migration in Long Island whaling diasporas. *Island Studies Journal*, *16*(1), 43–61.

Guo B (2006). 和谐社会诞生于解决社会矛盾的阵痛之中—论社会矛盾和社会和谐的辩证关系. 郑州大学学报:哲学社会科学版, *39*(2), 51–55.

Guo S (2017). 中国国际关系理论建设中的中国意识成长及中国学派前途. 国际观察, *145*(1), 19–39.

Hagström L, & Nordin AH (2020). China's "politics of harmony" and the quest for soft power in international politics. *International Studies Review*, *22*(3), 507–525.

Kavalski E (2018). Guanxi or what is the Chinese for relational theory of world politics. *China Political Science Review*, *18*(3), 233–251.

Kim HJ (2016). Will IR theory with Chinese characteristics be a powerful alternative? *The Chinese Journal of International Politics*, *9*(1), 59–79.

Korson C, Poaouteta S, & Prinsen G (2020). Triangular negotiations of island sovereignty: Indigenous and customary authorities-metropolitan states-local metropolitan authorities. *Island Studies Journal*, *15*(1), 67–88.

Ling LHM (2017). World politics in colour. *Millennium*, *45*(3), 473–491.

Meyer MA (2001). Our own liberation: Reflections on Hawaiian epistemology. *The Contemporary Pacific*, *13*(1), 124–148.

Mignolo WD (2011). *The darker side of Western modernity*. Duke University Press.

Mignolo WD (2002). The enduring enchantment (or the epistemic privilege of modernity and where to go from here). *The South Atlantic Quarterly*, *101*(4), 927–954.

Murray C (2020). Imperial dialectics and epistemic mapping: From decolonisation to anti-Eurocentric IR. *European Journal of International Relations*, *26*(2), 419–442.

Nadarajah Y (2021). Future past I am a coolie-al . . . and I reside as an invisible island inside the ocean: Tidalectics, transoceanic crossings, coolitude and a Tamil identity. *Island Studies Journal*, *16*(1), 155–172.

Nadarajah Y, & Grydehøj A (2016). Island studies as a decolonial project. *Island Studies Journal*, *11*(2), 437–446.

Qin Y (2018). *A relational theory of world politics*. Cambridge University Press.

Rodd A (2020). A road to island sovereignty and empowerment? Fiji's aims within the Belt and Road Initiative. *Island Studies Journal*, *15*(2), 93–118.

Ruíz E (2020). Cultural gaslighting. *Hypatia*, *35*(4), 687–713.

Smith G, & Wesley-Smith T (2021). *The China alternative: Changing regional order in the Pacific Islands*. Australian National University Press.

Szadziewski H (2020). Converging anticipatory geographies in Oceania: The Belt and Road Initiative and look north in Fiji. *Political Geography*, *77*, 102119.

Todd Z (2016). An Indigenous feminist's take on the ontological turn: "Ontology" is another word for colonialism. *Journal of Historical Sociology*, *29*(1), 1–22.

Tuck E, & Yang KW (2012). Decolonization is not a metaphor. *Education & Society*, *1*(1), 1–40.

Wang Z (2006). 关于新闻宣传与和谐社会的两点思考. 岭南新闻探索, (F01), 22–23.

Xie B, Zhu X, & Grydehøj A (2020). Perceiving the Silk Road Archipelago: Archipelagic relations within the ancient and 21st-century Maritime Silk Road. *Island Studies Journal, 15*(2), 55–72.

Xu J (2015). 新天下主义与中国的内外秩序. *知识分子论丛, 13*(1), 3–25.

Yan X (2019). *Leadership and the rise of great powers*. Princeton University Press.

Yan X (2013). *Ancient Chinese thought, modern Chinese power*. Princeton University Press.

Yusoff K (2018). *A billion black Anthropocenes or none*. University of Minnesota Press.

Zhang Y (2015). China and the struggle for legitimacy of a rising power. *The Chinese Journal of International Politics, 8*(3), 301–322.

Zhao T (2009). A political world philosophy in terms of all-under-heaven (Tian-xia). *Diogenes, 56*(1), 5–18.

Zhou Z (2007). 构建社会主义和谐社会必须走出四个认识误区. *前沿, 224*(6), 148–150.

3 Harmony in traditional Chinese thought

Conceptions of harmony in Confucian, Mohist, and Taoist traditions

When Chinese IR theorists discuss harmony, they usually ground the concept in ancient Chinese thought. The theories have been constructed to address today's world politics, yet these theorists are keen to demonstrate continuity with the past. However, ancient Chinese thought was vast, varied, and developed in a cumulative manner over the course of many centuries. Its societal influence was furthermore successively altered and reoriented at various times in imperial and 20th-century China. It is thus impossible to provide a straightforward definition of the ancient Chinese concept of harmony. Because we wish to understand what harmony means for Chinese IR theorists today, however, it is necessary to briefly consider the varied notions concerning harmony in ancient and imperial China.

Harmony evidently played a foundational role in ancient Chinese culture. The character for *he* (和 harmony) appears in late Shang dynasty (1300s–1000s BCE) inscriptions in turtle shell, bone, and bronze.[1] The ancient historiographer Shi Bo (史伯) ascribes the decline of the late Western Zhou dynasty (1045–771 BCE) to its rulers' pursuit of *tong* (同 uniformity, homogeneity) instead of harmony:

> Harmony gives rise to new things. Uniformity leads to stagnation. Balancing one thing with another is called harmony. This is how to flourish, endure, and bring things together. Adding to the same thing yet more of the same thing will ruin the whole.[2]

Here, harmony is a unity of contradiction and difference and is achievable only through the cultivation of diversity.

In the Spring and Autumn period (770–476 BCE), Confucius (孔子, 551–479 BCE) regarded harmony as a moral requirement: while noble people

DOI: 10.4324/9781003259794-3

pursue harmony instead of uniformity, petty or small-minded people pursue uniformity instead of harmony.[3] From this perspective, harmony is the state of diversity and a fusion between different things. The harmony of differences, when applied to the modern world of multiple societies and civilisations, is seen by some as involving recognition of and respect for different ethnic groups and countries.[4] Even if ancient Chinese rulers did not always follow this advice, most dominant streams of ancient Chinese thought advocate peaceful coexistence among nations and oppose military conquest of other states. This has proven an appealing set of foundations for present-day Chinese IR theorists.

This is, however, just one interpretation. In traditional Chinese thought, *hexie* can refer to inner harmony, harmony among people, and harmony between people and the universe. The Confucian classic *Shangshu* (尚书 *Esteemed Documents*), written in the late Warring States period (475–221 BCE), describes harmony in this manner: "[King] Yao kept his clans close and in harmony by promoting his own intelligence and virtues, distinguishing between good and evil of his clan leaders, as well as uniting and harmonising the myriad states, which thereby transformed all people and resulted in great harmony under heaven."[5] Confucian harmony involves a willingness to select some things and not others, to differentiate and not treat everything the same, regardless of virtue and ability.

Zhouli (周礼 *Rites of the Zhou*), a canonical work of Confucianism concerning Western Zhou bureaucracy and organisational theory, emphasises how it is through the constitution of customs (礼 *li*) that "the states are harmonised, the officials brought into accord, and the peoples united in concord."[6] Harmony here is enforced by rules of proper conduct, which help keep society and heaven in balance. This idea is also prominent in *Liji* (礼记 *Book of Rites*), a compilation of Warring States period and early Han dynasty (202 BCE–CE 9) texts, which presents the Zhou dynasty as a golden age, a state of "great harmony under heaven" (天下大同 *tianxia datong*).[7]

The important Confucian thinker Mencius (孟子, 372–289 BCE) recommends an ideal social state of harmony in which one is "to care for one's own aged parents and then extend the same care to other old people in general; to love one's own children and then extend the same love to other children in general."[8] For both Confucius and Mencius, proper familial relations provide a model for an individual's relations with other social actors of varying degrees of intimacy, but this does not mean that care for strangers is weighted equally with care for family members. That, however, is precisely the approach of the influential thinker Mozi (墨子, c. 476–c. 390 BCE). Mozi argues in favour of *jianxiangai* (兼相爱 impartial mutual care) and *shangtong* (尚同 exalting unity). His radical proposition is that true harmony lies in extending absolute care to everyone, equally.

Laozi (老子, c. 571–c. 471 BCE), a Taoist thinker and reputed author of *Daodejing* (道德经 *Book of the Tao and Its Virtue*), describes an ideal society as one characterised by *wuyu* (无欲 no desire), *wuwei* (无为 no action, things take their own course), and *wuzheng* (无争 no contention) among people. In such a society, all people, "satisfied with their food, clothes, housing, and customs" live in harmony and with tolerance for one another.[9] Zhuangzi (庄子, c. 369–c. 286 BCE), another significant Taoist thinker, advocates a world of harmony between human beings and all of existence, in which "heaven, the world, and I were produced together, and all things and I are one."[10] In line with wider Taoist principles, virtue lies in decisive action designed to preclude the need for future decision and action. *Tao* (道 the way) is the goal of the virtuous person, but it is a goal that is self-defeating. *Tao* is the way things are and the direction in which the universe flows in the absence of deviant behaviour.

This fundamental idea of Taoism is frequently illustrated by the *taijitu* (太极图), known in English as the *yin-yang* symbol. The harmony of the universe can be achieved through the balance of *yin* (阴 dark, feminine, negative) and *yang* (阳 bright, masculine, positive). *Yin* and *yang* are two complementary opposites that constantly restrain and create each other. Their interaction is one of dynamic equilibrium, not conflict. They are interdependent and mutually convertible. When *yin* waxes and *yang* wanes to the extreme point, *yin* will begin dwindling, and *yang* will begin growing, and vice versa.

The Taoist ideal of effortless harmonious flow differs from the Confucian ideal of harmonisation through sorting the good from the bad. Both differ in turn from the utilitarian Mohist ideal of assessing correct action on the basis of what brings about the best results for society or the world.

Elements of these divergent intellectual traditions influenced one another, and they developed in dialogue. For example, the *taijitu* has been significant as a tool for understanding ethics and cosmology in both Taoism and Confucianism. These schools of thought also mingled with other intellectual traditions connected with Buddhism (which began entering China from the Indian subcontinent in the first and second centuries CE)[11] and localised but mobile folk religions. This mixing process was itself a matter of debate. For example, the so-called neo-Confucianism movement of the Song dynasty (960–1279 CE) sought to disentangle Confucian traditions from those of Taoism and Buddhism, resulting in new formulations of Confucian ethics and metaphysics. Ironically, the efforts to remove religion from Confucianism led to strands of 11th- and 12th-century thought that recreated Confucianism as an alternative religion, perhaps reaching its pinnacle in the work of the influential scholar Zhu Xi (朱熹, 1130–1200 CE).[12]

These processes of mixing and separation, creation and renewal, ultimately resulted in a Chinese cultural emphasis on fostering harmony not just between different people but also between people, the world, and heaven. This characteristic spanned different traditions and schools of thought, even as harmony itself continued to hold conflicting meanings. Four basic characteristics of harmony have been identified as emerging out of ancient China: balance in the whole, coordination in difference, order in complexity, and unity in diversity.[13]

Useful though retrospective attempts to integrate the various ancient Chinese approaches to harmony may be, it is important to recognise that ancient Chinese traditions deployed harmony to very different ends, particularly in terms of their conclusions as to whose interests were worth harmonising. Much as in our metaphor of gardens, that which might appear harmonious to one person might appear chaotic to someone else. Harmony is open to varied interpretation. Recognition of the multitude of ways in which harmony has been understood over the past millennia perhaps contributes to, rather than challenges, the concept's centrality to Chinese thought.[14]

Notes

1 Li & Zhao 2012, 159.
2 qtd. in Yu 2010, 16.
3 Yang 1980, 141.
4 Wang & Jiang 2019, 129.
5 qtd. in Mu 2009, 2.
6 Lü 2004, 14.
7 Yang 2004, 265.
8 qtd. in Wan & Lan 2007, 14.
9 qtd. in Rao 2007, 190.
10 qtd. in Sun 2007, 20.
11 Wu 1994, 115.
12 Sterckx 2019, 316–324.
13 Wang 2019, 105.
14 Sterckx 2019, 209.

References

Li X, & Zhao P (2012). 字源: 上. 天津古籍出版社.
Lü Y (2004). 周礼译注. 中州古籍出版社.
Mu P (2009). 尚书. 中华书局.
Rao S (2007). 老子. 中华书局.
Sterckx R (2019). *Chinese thought: From Confucius to Cook Ding*. Penguin.
Sun T (2007). 庄子. 中华书局.
Wan L, & Lan X (2007). 孟子. 中华书局.

Wang J (2019). 以和为贵 和而不同—谈谈中国文化的和谐观. *中国领导科学*, *54*(3), 104–107.

Wang Q, & Jiang X (2019). 中国传统和谐观为什么历千年而弥新. *人民论坛*, *628*(11), 128–130.

Wu Z (1994). 关中早期佛教传播史料钩稽. *中国史研究*, *64*(4), 115–120.

Yang B (1980). 论语译注. 中华书局.

Yang T (2004). 礼记译注. 上海古籍出版社.

Yu KP (2010). The Confucian conception of harmony. In Tao J, Cheung ABL, Painter M, & Li C (Eds) *Governance for harmony in Asia and beyond* (15–36). Routledge.

4 Approaches to harmony in Chinese IR theory

Early developments in Chinese IR theory

Chinese IR scholarship is today a diverse and internationally engaged field. We focus here on three particular theoretical approaches that emphasise the concept of harmony. It must be borne in mind, however, that there are other approaches and traditions within Chinese IR theory as well.

The academic study of world politics in China began in the mid-1950s, and the geopolitical tumult of the late 1970s gave new impetus to the study of IR.[1] In his review of the history of Chinese IR, Xiao Ren argues that specifically Chinese IR theory has over the decades largely moved beyond early debates regarding tensions between ideology, policy analysis, and scholarly inquiry.[2] These debates had gained urgency due to the increasing influence of translations of European and especially American IR texts in Chinese universities in the 1990s.[3]

Since the start of the 2000s, Chinese IR scholarship has placed growing emphasis on distinguishing itself from Western theoretical traditions.[4] Qin Yaqing, whose work we discuss in detail later, systematically differentiates his approach from the Western 'mainstream' IR theory within structural realism, neoliberal institutionalism, and structural constructivism.[5] Qin argues that "mainstream IR theory has a common and commensurable metaphysical component in its theoretical hard core—ontological individualism," which differs essentially from Chinese theory.[6] Regardless of whether Chinese theory and Western theory are essentially different, it is significant that many Chinese IR theorists believe this to be the case.

Harmony was identified early on as a valuable perspective for Chinese IR research. The prominent IR scholars Yu Zheng and Chen Yugang advocated a theory of global co-governance (全球共治 *quanqiu gongzhi*) in the early 2000s. This helped set the stage for later and more complex theorisations of harmonious IR. Yu and Chen are less interested in the structure

DOI: 10.4324/9781003259794-4

and machinery of global governance than in identifying the best *practice* of global co-governance. They argue that global co-governance can be achieved only by "implementing the Doctrine of the Mean on a global scale. The Doctrine of the Mean takes 'harmony' as its goal and 'middle' as its way."[7] Walking the middle (中 *zhong*) path is a method of navigating between the extremes of globalism and nationalism.[8]

Yu and Chen's approach calls for a constant balancing and harmonisation of behaviour. They apply this to relations between polities:

> Advocating a culture of "harmony" is the best way to resolve global conflicts and promote global cooperation and co-governance. Its cornerstone is Mozi's notion of "impartial mutual care, impartial mutual benefit." . . . Everything should follow the principle of "benefiting others": Everyone tries to benefit others so as to achieve equal participation, co-governance, and shared prosperity. . . . Maintenance of lasting and harmonious co-existence of different groups requires global co-governance rooted in the six core concepts of traditional Chinese culture: . . . the cosmology of the unity of heaven and humankind; humanistic benevolence and love; a developmental perspective integrating *yin* and *yang*; a practical perspective on the unity of knowing and doing; a cultural approach of pluralism and compatibility; and valuing the unity of justice, interests, and harmony.[9]

This use of ancient Chinese thought is striking, given Western IR theory's tendency to take its foundational logic as universal. Yu and Chen draw upon a mix of ancient Chinese intellectual traditions, including Mohism, Confucianism, and Taoism. For example, Yu and Chen present the Confucian doctrine of the mean (中庸 *zhongyong*) as the overarching philosophy of global co-governance but ground global co-governance practice in Taoist dualism and the key Mohist concept of "impartial mutual care, impartial mutual benefit" (兼相爱,交相利 *jianxiang'ai, jiaoxiangli*). However, Mohism's advocacy of impartial care was historically developed as a critical response to the embrace of strict hierarchies of love, which are so evident in Confucian thought and which find expression in the doctrine of the mean. At the same time, recourse to Taoist cosmology results in ambiguity as to whether global co-governance is the natural state of relations between polities or whether it is a goal to which polities should aspire.

Such critique is probably beside the point. Yu and Chen's concept of global co-governance was not designed as a coherent contribution to Chinese philosophy. It was designed to stake a claim for Chinese perspectives on world politics.

Although Yu and Chen's early 2000s approach did not amount to a full-fledged IR theory, it set precedents that later, more sophisticated Chinese IR theories followed:

1   It presents itself as rooted in ancient Chinese tradition;
2   It emphasises harmony;
3   It straddles the line between being a theory for describing world politics and a theory for perfecting the practice of world politics;
4   It purports to be applicable to world politics as a whole, but its embeddedness in explicitly Chinese thought could imply Chinese exceptionalism;
5   It focuses on the practice of relations between polities, on relationality *per se.*

All three of the Chinese IR theories that we consider in detail in the following sections have continued along these lines, even as they have moved in different directions.

Our literature search showed that, of the numerous schools of IR theory that have emerged in China since the early 2000s, three of the most prominent present themselves as rooted in traditional Chinese conceptions of harmony and seek to provide specifically Chinese and relational perspectives on world politics. These theories are *tianxia* (天下 all-under-heaven), *guanxi* (关系 relational), and *gongsheng* (共生 symbiosis).

Another of the most prominent theories, Yan Xuetong's *daoyi* (道义 moral) theory, likewise grounds itself in ancient Chinese thought but is not explicitly relational. More significantly for the present study, *daoyi* theory bases itself "on the realist assumptions of strength, power and national interest" and regards "national political leadership and national power as the two decisive factors determining a state's foreign strategy orientation."[10] Because *daoyi* theory does not emphasise harmony, we do not devote attention to it here.

Tianxia theory

Recognised as a major Chinese school of IR thinking, *tianxia* (天下 all-under-heaven) theory was introduced by the philosopher Zhao Tingyang.[11]

Zhao's *tianxia* theory builds upon the work of Ye Zicheng, who compares Western IR with ancient Chinese diplomacy.[12] Ye argues that the mid to late Spring and Autumn period (770–476 BCE) and subsequent Warring States period (475–221 BCE) were characterised by interaction between sovereign states. These states possessed independent political power, clear territorial demarcations and population divisions, the right to independently carry out internal and foreign affairs, and shared norms for interstate relations. Terms such as *tianxia*, *sihai* (四海 the four seas), and *qianshengzhiguo* (千乘之国

state with a thousand chariots) appear repeatedly in the Confucian classics, revealing a contemporary conception of international relations.[13] Harmony was an ideal for existence in general and interstate relations in particular and could be achieved through custom and the doctrine of the mean.[14] Other scholars follow Ye in applying Confucian IR to Chinese diplomacy, emphasising the idea of great harmony under heaven (天下大同 *tianxia datong*) as the ideal social order.[15]

During the war-torn Spring and Autumn and Warring States periods, Chinese thinkers often used the early Zhou dynasty as a 'golden age' role model. Zhao does the same, using Zhou dynasty thinking to diagnose a modern failure in recognising the world as world:

> Our supposed *world* is still a non-world. This side of creation, our globe, has not yet become a world of oneness, but remains a Hobbes-ian *chaos*, since there is no truly coherent world society governed by a universally-accepted political institution. Politically abandoned, the world we live in, in a geographical sense, is the only one we have. A lack of political unity means that a universal political identity is still nowhere to be found. Such a world is impossible unless it is organized and controlled by a worldwide institution, itself based upon a global political philosophy.[16]

In Zhao's reformulation of the ancient concept, *tianxia* can be understood at three levels: physical world, psychological world, and institutional world.[17] We can understand the world only at the global scale, not at the subordinate national scale. Zhao's *tianxia* rests upon the principle of excluding nothing and no one (无外原则 *wuwai yuanze*):[18] *tianxia* must include all peoples and all lands. There is no 'foreign' or 'domestic', no 'self' or 'other'. Our ability to conceive of a thing and our ability to order a thing are inseparable. Because states are subordinate parts of the world, efforts at statecraft are doomed to failure:

> The political concept of "nation" is familiar to all, since we all know what needs to be done for the nation-state. However, it is not so for the political notion of "world," since people are unaware of what should be done for the latter. The key problem today is that of a *failed world* as opposed to that of so-called *failed states*. No country could possibly be successful in a failed world.[19]

This echoes Mozi's argument that people fail to act in a manner that benefits everyone because they fail to understand their true relationship with others. Both selfish and statist behaviour result from mistaking the part for the whole. This intellectual tradition also links back to the Taoist notion that correct knowledge naturally produces correct action.

The appropriate focus of world politics is not 'internationality' but 'worldness'.[20] As Zhao writes, "The world's universal wellbeing takes priority over that of the nation-state."[21] This is not a 'world system' of imperial dominance or hegemony. It is not the application of harmony through force. Rulership *over* the world differs from worldness: "The world *is* only when so justified; and to be justified, a political system of universal 'harmony' needs to be developed, so as to successfully solve the problem of universal cooperation between all peoples."[22] *Tianxia* does not rule all; it *is* all.

Tianxia is a process of harmony, diversity, and cooperation. This process is not incompatible with the current international system of sovereign states, but it can be achieved only if it rises above these states. Zhao distinguishes between "philosophy *for* the world and philosophy *of* the world":

> Anybody can have a world philosophy in accordance with his own horizons. Likewise, any nation can have a world philosophy in keeping with national interests. However, we need a world philosophy which speaks on behalf of the world. The world is absent because of our refusal to see it from its own perspective. The failure of world politics is essentially the failure of philosophy. The question is therefore how to take care of the world *for the world*?[23]

Thinking with the world naturally produces a world institution of governance. An overarching strategy of harmony (和策略 *hecelue*) thus relies on world-oriented approaches, such as mutual imitation strategy (普遍的策略模仿 *pubian de celue mofang*), in which actors follow one another's best practices, and Confucian improvement (孔子改进 *kongzi gaijin*), in which actors always gain more by cooperating than they could possibly gain by acting independently.[24] *Tianxia* theory envisions a world institution capable of maintaining world peace, interests, and order for all peoples, harmoniously and equally.[25] This world institution is all-encompassing rather than absolute.

Tianxi is ultimately a framework for harmoniously carrying out national and local governance:

> Harmony is the necessary ontological condition for different things to exist and develop, usually defined as reciprocal dependence, reciprocal improvement or the perfect fitting for different things, as opposed to the *sameness* of things. . . . Harmony as opposed to sameness is basically speaking a question of multiplicity rather than oneness.[26]

Zhao's "philosophical renewal" of the *tianxia* concept[27] has prompted significant debate within Chinese academia, in part because of its forerunner status as an IR theory that is both explicitly Chinese and intended to be globally applicable. Philosopher Gan Chunsong commends the theory for presenting an ideal political order and for identifying state-centricism's failure to serve the world's people. Gan nevertheless suggests that, much like Zhou dynasty *tianxia* thinking, Zhao's *tianxia* is more a critical discourse than a challenge to the existing international system.[28] Others, in contrast, see *tianxia* as inescapably utopian.[29]

Feng Weijiang feels *tianxia* theory could be put into practice through a global mechanism for cooperation and shared expectations at multiple levels of government.[30] Taking a Confucian approach, Li Mingming criticises Zhao's *tianxia* for focusing on systems of governance or 'political doctrine' (政道 *zhengdao*) instead of on methods of governance or 'governmental doctrine' (治道 *zhidao*).[31] Zhou Fangyin suggests that *tianxia*'s vision of a single institutional model cannot offer effective solutions at all levels of world governance.[32]

Xu Jianxin questions the usefulness of Zhao's idealist philosophy research methods and what Xu sees as his superficial examination of ancient Chinese *tianxia* thinking and practice.[33] Given that *tianxia* theory has, as we shall see, been singled out by some Western scholars as expressing a Chinese desire to exert imperial dominance, this critique of Zhao's perceived lack of interest in the actual historical use of *tianxia* should be taken seriously.

Sympathetic scholars generally see *tianxia* theory as providing a framework for transcending presumptions of competition, victory, and loss in world politics, transforming today's competitors into tomorrow's partners. What is lacking is a practical road map to creating a world institution capable of achieving peace and harmony. Zhao in a sense suggests that *tianxia* emerges out of awareness of *tianxia*: when we know the world, we act in a worldly manner.

As in Yu and Chen's theory of global co-governance, it is possible to see Zhao's *tianxia* theory less as an expounding of ancient Chinese wisdom and experience and more as a combination of select parts of diverse intellectual traditions. There are Taoist conceptualisations of an ordered universe and of the unity of knowledge and practice, the Mohist insistence on a universal duty to care, and explicitly Confucian discussions of strategic behaviour and proper hierarchies.

Tianxia theory's perspective on world politics is overtly Chinese, but it is a perspective from above. *Tianxia* theory is a way of seeing the whole world at once, but as a result, it is lacking in detail. It is not particularly interested in the relations that particular actors have with one another. If we think of

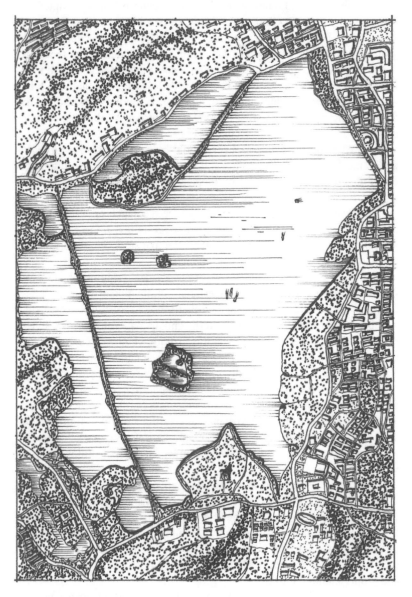

Figure 4.1 A bird's-eye view, seeing everything equally from a great distance.

Source: Lin Guangyu, 2021.

our classical Chinese garden, we can imagine *tianxia* theory as a bird's-eye view: high above, seeing everything equally from a great distance.

Guanxi theory

Guanxi (关系 relational) theory was developed by Qin Yaqing. This theory takes its starting point in a posited opposition between 'Western' and 'Chinese' ways of thinking and acting, which are influenced by distinct sets of 'background knowledge'. These differing perspectives cause Western IR theory to "prioritize the ontology of existence" and thereby emphasise individual entities and their self-existence, self-interest, and egoistic action. In contrast, Chinese thought focuses on relatedness, coexistence, and the "existence of the self in relation to others rather than existence in isolation."[34]

From Qin's Chinese perspective, all social actors (including polities) are relational, and the world itself consists of relations. This affects our perceptions of choice and strategic activity:

> The logic of relationality holds that an actor makes judgments and decisions according to her relationships to specific others, with the totality of her relational circles or the relational context as the background. In any social setting, what action an actor is to take depends very much on her relationships with specific others and her relations with the relational context in which she is embedded. In other words, her interests, desires, and preferences . . . change as the nature of a relationship changes.[35]

Zhao's *tianxia* theory sees all interests as shared by all peoples and states through a network of universal and uniform relatedness and equality of difference. In contrast, drawing upon the classic scholarship of Fei Xiaotong,[36] Qin regards all interests, identities, and powers as constructed through an actor's relations with other actors. Coexistence and existence are mutually constitutive; the one does not precede or deny the other.[37] As Qin writes, this is best illustrated through

> the meta-relationship between *yin* and *yang* in the Chinese *zhongyong* dialectics . . . *Yin* and *yang* are opposites in unity and their interaction is not only intersubjective but also immanent, for they are by definition within each other. . . . Any power the self (*yin*) has is at the same time shared by the other (*yang*).[38]

Yu and Chen's global co-governance and Zhao's *tianxia* theories use the doctrine of the mean (中庸 *zhongyong*) primarily as a strategy for finding the most mutually beneficial solutions. Qin, however, presents *zhongyong* dialectics in terms of harmony as process, almost as an epistemology in itself. Rather than conceiving of political actors as independent entities trapped in existential conflict, *guanxi* theory sees them as mutually constituted and mutually empowered relators. *Guanxi* theory emphasises relationships of reciprocity in which actors raise themselves by benefiting others, highlighting Confucius' adage, "If you want to establish yourself, help others to establish themselves; if you want to be successful, help others to be successful."[39] For Qin, rationality is necessarily secondary to relation, given that the self cannot exist without others: "Egoistic rationality based upon the ontology of the isolated self-existence is likely to be irrational once it is put in a coexistent context. . . . Interest is shared because it is defined first of all in a relational context."[40] There can be no rational self-interest, just relational shared interest.

Qin's *guanxi* theory and his ambition to establish distinctively Chinese approaches to IR have had a major impact on Chinese IR research.[41] Su Changhe argues that the traditional Chinese wisdom of comprehensive understanding (会通 *huitong*) is indispensable to *guanxi* theory, that relational choice should replace rational choice for understanding world politics, and that *guanxi* theory is useful for studying connections between China and the world.[42] Gao Shangtao advances *guanxi zhuyi* (关系主义 relationalism) as an analytical framework for Chinese IR research and details its ontology, epistemology, and logic.[43] Gao's *guanxi zhuyi* theory uses Qin's work as the basis for a new approach to practicing world politics: *guanxi zhuyi* seeks to reorient the existing international system toward sovereign states that insist on relational rationality and practice the Confucian strategy of benevolence and righteousness (仁义 *ren yi*). This will foster relations of optimal coexistence between states and the maximal realisation of shared interests. As a theory of world politics, *guanxi zhuyi* understands national problems as processes within a structure of sovereign relational coexistence.

Cao Dejun deploys social network analysis to conceptualise the formation of trust in world politics.[44] Cao argues that trust embedded within international social networks arises from relations between actors: relational networks produce trust, while trust strengthens or weakens relational networks. As trust is established, it is institutionalised, disseminated, and internalised, thereby affecting actors' attributes and behaviours. Because relational networks are dynamic and may involve asymmetric dependence, trust allocates resources in the form of social capital. Cao Dejun and Chen Jinli elsewhere present an analytical framework for network theory combined with relational ontology.[45] Xie Baoxia, Zhu Xianlong, and Adam Grydehøj advocate use of *guanxi* theory to perceive less conflictual relationships between disparate polities and to subvert binary thinking.[46]

Ji Ling maintains that globalisation and technological change have heightened interrelatedness and fluidity in world politics and have driven scholars from different cultural backgrounds toward relational ontologies and relational turns.[47] Relationality transcends East-West binaries and promotes truly global IR research. Ji highlights the need for vigilance regarding the epistemological traps of reification and binary opposition as well as recognition of the variability of the relational world and individuals' immanent relatedness with one another and with the whole. The fact that many Western approaches are also termed 'relational' furthermore causes difficulty in communicating Qin's theory as a distinct contribution to the international scholarship.

Shang Huipeng raises a number of fundamental questions regarding Qin's *guanxi* theory: is Confucianism truly generalisable in terms of relationality? Have Western structural realism, neoliberal institutionalism, and structural constructivism truly ignored interstate relations? Is an actor's behaviour entirely determined by its relations? Are rationality and relationality genuinely conceptual opposites?[48] Shang also criticises *guanxi* theory's emphasis on shifting processes (rather than on definitive conclusions and causal connections) as insufficient for explaining real-world problems.

Guanxi theory's perspective is one at ground level. It sees the world as an individual person would see it, focusing on that one person's relationships with other people and things. *Guanxi* theory is attentive to the details of world politics as they relate to specific social actors and the other social actors with which they relate. In terms of our Chinese garden, *guanxi* theory is a view from the edge of the lake: the highly personal view of an individual in constant interaction with their environment.

Gongsheng theory

Gongsheng (共生 symbiosis) theory emerged in the early 2010s. *Gongsheng* researchers can be divided into two groups. The first group, including scholars such as Jin Yingzhou (2011), Hu Shoujun (2012), and Cai Liang (2015), combines classical Marxism with traditional Chinese discourses of harmony to apply *gongsheng* (a term derived from biology) to the analysis of world politics.[49] Such studies have focused on the evolution of Chinese diplomacy over time, with little reference to Western IR theory.

The second group, including Ren Xiao and Su Changhe, explicitly seeks to offer an alternative to Western IR.[50] These scholars use ancient Chinese diplomatic practice and political thought to explore the historical significance of a symbiotic international system in ancient East Asia. These historical lessons encourage the present-day construction of a symbiotic international system to replace the Western-dominated system.

Figure 4.2 A view from ground level, focused on an individual's interaction with their environment.

Source: Lin Guangyu, 2021.

Ren and Su are responding in part to the influence of John King Fairbank's influential 1942 conceptualisation of a tributary (朝贡 *chaogong*) system in which China represented the centre of the traditional East Asian international order prior to the arrival of Western colonialism.[51] Ren contends that the traditional East Asian order was instead characterised by symbiosis, by a *gongsheng* system in which countries—whether large or small, strong or weak—could find a proper place and which over the course of millennia formed a set of principles, norms, and codes of conduct for managing interstate relations. This polycentric traditional East Asian system fostered multiple modes of interaction, tribute trade, voluntary exchanges, peaceful coexistence, and shared legitimacy, which distinguished it from international systems elsewhere in the world.[52] Su calls for further research into the traditional *gongsheng* system in order to counter the tributary approach, which continues to negatively affect overseas understandings of present-day Chinese diplomacy and international activity.[53]

Drawing heavily upon traditional Chinese thought, especially Confucianism, the second group of *gongsheng* scholars emphasises the pluralistic nature of the world and argue that ideological and cultural homogenisation are both undesirable and impossible. For Ren, "*Gongsheng* theory is built on differences and diversity rather than sameness between and among things" and is based on four fundamental assumptions: 1) "The nature of the world is pluralism," 2) "There are all kinds of differences between and among things," 3) "Different things can peacefully or even amicably coexist and interact with each other on the basis of equality," and 4) "Different things, through constructive interactions, can together achieve advancement."[54]

Within this framework, states should seek symbiotic peace, harmony, inclusiveness, and cooperation rooted in acceptance of difference. The *gongsheng* system sees states as mutually dependent, not merely coexistent. While *gongsheng*'s focus on mutual dependence resembles parts of Zhao's *tianxia* theory, the *gongsheng* approach does not assume symbiosis as a universal attribute. Symbiosis should instead be the goal of international society: cooperation and harmony are superior to competition and chaos. *Gongsheng* theory does not see a *tianxia*-style world government as the solution:

> "Symbiotic peace" simply is peace through symbiotic means. In such a situation, [sovereign states] relate with one another and grow together symbiotically. Their robust coexistence and parallel growth does not require them to become the same, but rather to allow and respect the various differences among them.[55]

Advocates of *gongsheng* theory often regard China as a unique international actor and emphasise China's potential for creating a symbiotic international system.[56] *Gongsheng* theory has been applied to various research areas within IR, prominently including studies of the China-USA relationship, stressing the significance of symbiotic harmony with mutual respect, win-win cooperation, equality, mutual trust, inclusivity, and mutual learning.[57] Cai Liang argues that a symbiotic international system could be divided into three stages (peaceful coexistence, peaceful symbiosis, and harmonious symbiosis): within this framework, China is actively conceptualising peaceful symbiosis and preparing for harmonious symbiosis, including the creation of a community of common destiny (人类命运共同体 *renlei mingyun gongtongti*) and a harmonious world (和谐世界 *hexie shijie*).[58] Yang Luhui envisions an East Asian community of common destiny that constructs new types of partnerships with win-win cooperation and with a symbiotic order that solves China's security dilemmas.[59] Huang Liqun creates a symbiotic evaluation system to measure degrees of mutual influence, interaction, and integration in terms of politics, economy, and culture among countries, specifically applying the system to assess the symbiotic qualities of the China-ASEAN community and to inform the construction of a closer China-ASEAN community of common destiny.[60] Liang Yin and Huang Liqun see a symbiotic international order as necessary for humanity's long-term peaceful and cooperative development. Symbiosis, rather than mere cooperation, is vital because the construction of a community of common destiny has no fixed end point but is a continual and unending process. Symbiosis involves pursuit of a balanced distribution of interests, mutual tolerance, respect for others' cultures, and equality of rights and obligations.[61] *Gongsheng* theory has also been used to study security issues, the Belt and Road Initiative, and other topics.[62]

Lu Lingyu criticises *gongsheng* theory for lacking an empirical basis, given that the *gongsheng* system existed only in the past and only in East Asia.[63] Zhang Feng calls for greater care in focusing study of historical international relations on an "incomplete [tribute] system that was constantly revised, challenged, or avoided by different actors. It was far from the totality of China's foreign relations, not to mention regional relations as a whole."[64] Lu Peng questions the logic of this theoretical practice and the relevance of Chinese thought to IR: is it useful to explain today's global problems by using elements of ancient or even modern Chinese thinking?[65] More generally, though, in Chinese scholarship, *gongsheng* theory has come to be seen as a less idealistic and more practical approach to guiding relationships between states than either the *tianxia* or *guanxi* theories.

Gongsheng theory's perspective is neither that of *tianxia* theory's bird's-eye view (seeing everything equally) nor that of *guanxi* theory's individual observer (creating their sense of self in relation to their environment). The bird's-eye view perceives a unitary world politics, while the individual

Figure 4.3 A view from atop a pagoda, extensive and impersonal, but still limited.
Source: Lin Guangyu, 2021.

observer's view perceives an array of bilateral relations between self and other.

In contrast, *gongsheng* theory looks at the world from above, but from an angle. It does not attempt to see the whole at once, but neither is it content with considering polity-to-polity relations one at a time. It instead seeks detailed understandings of particular sets of processes among a large number of particular social actors. If *gongsheng* theory were a view of the Chinese garden, it would be a view from atop the pagoda: extensive and impersonal, but still limited. Like the ground-level perspective of *guanxi* theory, it is a view that changes depending on where one decides to look, but like *tianxia* theory, the observer is not fully implicated in the scene being observed. The observer atop the pagoda is inside the garden, yet they do not simply see the garden as an extension of the relational self.

In the next chapter, we will consider how harmony-oriented Chinese IR theories relate to Chinese society.

Notes

1 Kim 2016; Song 2001; Su & Peng 1999.
2 Ren 2020.
3 Wang & Han 2016; Qin 2007.
4 Ren 2020; Su 2009; Guo 2017; Qin 2020, 2019; Acharya & Buzan 2017.
5 Qin 2018, 75–103.
6 Qin 2018, 75.
7 Yu & Chen 2005, 14.
8 Yu & Chen 2005, 14.
9 Yu & Chen 2005, 15.
10 Yan 2014; see also Yan 2019, 2016, 2013.
11 Zhao 2015, 2010, 2009a, 2009b, 2008, 2005.
12 Ye 2005, 2003; Ye & Pang 2001.
13 Ye 2003, 150.
14 Ye & Pang 2001, 26.
15 Chen 2008; Wang 2011; Sheng 2012; Jin & Chen 2020.
16 Zhao 2009a, 5.
17 Zhao 2005, 41–44.
18 Zhao 2005, 49–61.
19 Zhao 2009a, 5.
20 Zhao 2009b, 80–85.
21 Zhao 2009a, 6.
22 Zhao 2009a, 6.
23 Zhao 2009a, 7.
24 Zhao 2009b, 18, 119.
25 Zhao 2009b, 320–321.
26 Zhao 2009a, 14.
27 Zhao 2009a, 9.
28 Gan 2013, 2011, 2008.
29 Liu & Wang 2011; Zhang 2011.

30 Feng 2011.
31 Li 2011.
32 Zhou 2008.
33 Xu 2007.
34 Qin 2018, 121–123.
35 Qin 2018, 207–208.
36 Fei 1992.
37 Qin 2018, 139.
38 Qin 2018, 284–285.
39 qtd. in Yang 1980.
40 Qin 2018, 139.
41 Su 2009; Yang 2012; Wang 2015.
42 Su 2016a.
43 Gao 2010.
44 Cao 2010.
45 Cao & Chen 2011.
46 Xie, Zhu, & Grydehøj 2020.
47 Ji 2019.
48 Shang 2017.
49 Jin 2011; Hu 2012; Cai 2015.
50 Ren 2019, 2016, 2015, 2013; Su 2016b, 2013.
51 Fairbank 1942.
52 Ren 2013, 23.
53 Su 2016b.
54 Ren 2020, 20–21.
55 Ren 2020, 22.
56 Lu 2018.
57 Xia 2017; Liu & Ye 2019.
58 Cai 2014.
59 Yang 2017.
60 Huang 2016.
61 Liang & Huang 2017.
62 Liu & Ouyang 2019; Yao 2019; Xia 2015; Wang 2018.
63 Lu 2016.
64 Zhang 2015, 8.
65 Lu 2019.

References

Acharya A, & Buzan B (2017). Why is there no non-Western international relations theory? Ten years on. *International Relations of the Asia-Pacific*, *17*(3), 341–370.

Cai L (2015). 共生视角下"中国责任"的目标、实践及保证. 国际观察, *137*(5), 93–103.

Cai L (2014). 共生国际体系的优化: 从和平共处到命运共同体. 社会科学, *409*(9), 22–31.

Cao D (2010). 国家间信任的生成: 进程导向的社会网络分析. 当代亚太, *173*(5), 105–126.

Cao D, & Chen J (2011). 国际政治的关系网络理论: 一项新的分析框架. *欧洲研究*, *29*(4), 69–82.

Chen S (2008). *儒家文明与中国传统对外关系*. 山东大学出版社.

Fairbank JK (1942). Tributary trade and China's relations with the West. *The Journal of Asian Studies*, *1*(2), 129–149.

Fei X (1992). *From the soil: The foundations of Chinese society*. Hamilton GG, & Wang Z (Trans). University of California Press.

Feng W (2011). 试论"天下体系"的秩序特征、存亡原理及制度遗产. *世界经济与政治*, *372*(8), 4–29.

Gan C (2013). 王道理想的世界主义回归—儒家政治哲学与国际秩序再平衡. *人民论坛·学术前沿*, *27*(11), 37–48.

Gan C (2011). 王道理想与儒家世界秩序观的建构. *开放时代*, *228*(6), 44–57.

Gan C (2008). 世界和谐之愿景:《中庸》与儒家的"天下"观念. *学术月刊*, *40*(9), 50–56.

Gao S (2010). 关系主义与中国学派. *世界经济与政治*, *360*(8), 116–138.

Guo S (2017). 中国国际关系理论建设中的中国意识成长及中国学派前途. *国际观察*, *145*(1), 19–39.

Hu S (2012). 国际共生论. *国际观察*, *118*(4), 35–42.

Huang L (2016). 基于命运共同体建设的中国-东盟"共生度"评价. *广西民族研究*, *132*(6), 32–39.

Ji L (2019). 论"关系转向"的本体论自觉. *世界经济与政治*, *461*(1), 78–97.

Jin Y (2011). 为什么要研究"国际社会共生性"—兼议和平发展时代国际关系理论. *国际展望*, *14*(5), 1–17.

Jin Z, & Chen F (2020). 孔子外交思想的当代研究. *国际观察*, *163*(1), 101–118.

Kim HJ (2016). Will IR theory with Chinese characteristics be a powerful alternative? *The Chinese Journal of International Politics*, *9*(1), 59–79.

Li M (2011). 论天下思想中的政道与治道. *世界经济与政治*, *376*(12), 109–125.

Liang Y, & Huang L (2017). 共生型国际秩序与命运共同体建设. *南洋问题研究*, *169*(1), 39–50.

Liu H, & Wang C (2011). 论英国学派的国际秩序观—兼与天下体系理论的秩序观比较. *国际论坛*, *13*(6), 41–46.

Liu S, & Ye S (2019). 国际格局新型两极共生关系论析. *东北亚论坛*, *28*(2), 3–20.

Liu X, & Ouyang H (2019). 从共存安全到共生安全: 基于边境安全特殊性的思考. *国际安全研究*, *37*(2), 3–23.

Lu L (2016). 国际关系理论中国学派生成的路径选择. *欧洲研究*, *34*(5), 134–157.

Lu P (2019). 中国特色国际关系理论建设的阶段性进展与不足. *国际关系研究*, *40*(4), 74–83.

Lu P (2018). 理解中国国际关系理论的两种构建途径. *世界经济与政治*, *449*(1), 73–93.

Qin Y (2020). 全球国际关系学与中国国际关系理论. *国际观察*, *164*(2), 27–45.

Qin Y (2019). 中国国际关系理论的发展与贡献. *外交评论*, *180*(6), 1–10.

Qin Y (2018). *A relational theory of world politics*. Cambridge University Press.

Qin Y (2007). Why is there no Chinese international relations theory? *International Relations of the Asia-Pacific*, *7*(3), 313–340.

Ren X (2020). Grown from within: Building a Chinese school of international relations. *The Pacific Review*, *33*(3–4), 386–412.

Ren X (2019). *走向世界共生*. 商务印书馆.

Ren X (2016). 论国际共生的价值基础—对外关系思想和制度研究之三. *世界经济与政治*, *428*(4), 4–28.

Ren X (Ed) (2015). *共生: 上海学派的兴起*. 上海译文出版社.

Ren X (2013). 论东亚"共生体系"原理—对外关系思想和制度研究之一. *世界经济与政治*, *395*(7), 4–22.

Shang H (2017). 关于国际政治"关系理论"的几个问题—与秦亚青教授商榷. *社会科学文摘*, *20*(8), 31–33.

Sheng H (2012). 儒家的外交原则及其当代意义. *文化纵横*, *24*(4), 37–45.

Song X (2001). Building international relations theory with Chinese characteristics. *Journal of Contemporary China*, *10*(26), 61–74.

Su C (2016a). 关系理论的学术议程. *世界经济与政治*, *434*(10), 29–38.

Su C (2016b). 从关系到共生—中国大国外交理论的文化和制度阐释. *世界经济与政治*, *425*(1), 5–25.

Su C (2013). 共生型国际体系的可能—在一个多极世界中如何构建新型大国关系. *世界经济与政治*, *397*(9), 4–22.

Su C (2009). 当代中国国际关系理论:现状和发展. *国际展望*, *2*(2), 47–55.

Su C, & Peng Z (1999). 中国国际关系理论的贫困—对近二十年国际关系学在中国发展的反思. *世界经济与政治*, *86*(2), 15–19.

Wang C (2018). 钱学森开放复杂巨系统论视域下"一带一路"顶层设计研究. *学术探索*, *229*(12), 42–54.

Wang C (2015). 构建中国国际关系理论的大致路径—以秦亚青为个案的研究. *国际观察*, *134*(2), 71–80.

Wang R (2011). 孔子主义国际关系理论与中国外交. *现代国际关系*, *259*(5), 47–54.

Wang Y, & Han Z (2016). Why is there no Chinese IR theory? A cultural perspective. In Zhong Y, & Chang TC (Eds) *Constructing a Chinese school of international relations: Ongoing debates and sociological realities* (52–67). Routledge.

Xia L (2017). 全球共生系统理论与构建中美新型大国关系. *美国研究*, *31*(1), 21–45.

Xia L (2015). 论共生系统理论视阈下的"一带一路"建设. *同济大学学报(社会科学版)*, *26*(2), 30–40.

Xie B, Zhu X, & Grydehøj A (2020). Perceiving the Silk Road Archipelago: Archipelagic relations within the ancient and 21st-century Maritime Silk Road. *Island Studies Journal*, *15*(2), 55–72.

Xu J (2007). 天下体系与世界制度—评《天下体系:世界制度哲学导论》. *国际政治科学*, *10*(2), 113–142.

Yan X (2019). *Leadership and the rise of great powers*. Princeton University Press.

Yan X (2016). Political leadership and power redistribution. *The Chinese Journal of International Politics*, *9*(1), 1–26.

Yan X (2014). 道义现实主义的国际关系理论. *国际问题研究*, *163*(5), 102–128.

Yan X (2013). *Ancient Chinese thought, modern Chinese power*. Princeton University Press.

Yang B (1980). 论语译注. 中华书局.

Yang L (2017). 东亚命运共同体是合作共赢发展之盟. *社会主义研究*, *234*(4), 140–148.

Yang Y (2012). 中国国际关系理论研究 (2008–2011). *国际政治科学, 30*(2), 62–106.

Yao L (2019). 论国际关系中的"共生安全". *国际观察, 157*(1), 51–66.

Ye Z (2005). 中国外交的起源—试论春秋时期周王室和诸侯国的性质. *国际政治研究, 151*(1), 9–22.

Ye Z (2003). *春秋战国时期的中国外交思想*. 香港社会科学出版社有限公司.

Ye Z, & Pang X (2001). 中国春秋战国时期的外交思想流派及其与西方的比较. *世界经济与政治, 180*(12), 24–29.

Yu Z, & Chen Y (2005). 全球共治理论初探. *世界经济与政治, 234*(2), 8–15.

Zhang F (2015). *Chinese hegemony*. Stanford University Press.

Zhang F (2011). 天下体系: 一个中国式乌托邦中的世界秩序. *复旦国际关系评论, 1*, 87–92.

Zhao T (2015). 以天下重新定义政治概念:问题、条件和方法. *世界经济与政治, 418*(6), 4–22.

Zhao T (2010). 天下体系的现代启示. *文化纵横, 3*, 34–41.

Zhao T (2009a). A political world philosophy in terms of all-under-heaven (Tian-xia). *Diogenes, 56*(1), 5–18.

Zhao T (2009b). 坏世界研究: 作为第一哲学的政治哲学. 人民大学出版社.

Zhao T (2008). 天下体系的一个简要表述. *世界经济与政治, 262*(10), 57–65.

Zhao T (2005). 天下体系: 世界制度哲学导论. 江苏教育出版社.

Zhou F (2008). 天下体系是最好的世界制度吗?—再评《天下体系:世界制度哲学导论》. *国际政治科学, 14*(2), 98–104.

5 Using the past for the present

Traditions of change

The three harmony-oriented Chinese IR theories considered in this book are rhetorically grounded in ancient Chinese thought. The concept of harmony has, however, undergone constant reinvention, redefinition, and redeployment for new purposes throughout history.[1] Even in ancient China, thinkers and writers used "the past to explain and justify the present" and to address contemporary political needs.[2] Many of the extant ancient Chinese classics are compilations of works by numerous authors, who built upon, altered, honed, and redirected the arguments of their predecessors. Even the famous thinkers of the Spring and Autumn and Warring State periods often cast their ideas as reflections upon early (and by that point, part-mythical) Zhou dynasty thought and practice.[3]

This backward-looking tendency within Chinese scholarship both signals respect for tradition and is a means of calling into question prevailing theories, doctrines, and ideologies without disrupting the fundamentals of society. Creative use of history in present-day scholarship is itself a technique for maintaining harmony. A rhetoric of continuity offers a veneer of familiarity to even innovative or challenging ideas. In present-day Chinese IR scholarship, attentiveness to the past is partially about inspiring visions of alternative futures in an easily graspable and politically praiseworthy manner.

The politically sensitive balance between past and present is evident in the literature's terminological shifts. Although all three theories considered here are grounded in ideas of harmony, the term *hexie* peaked in popularity in the Chinese IR literature in the mid-2000s, after then-president Hu Jintao introduced the *hexie shijie* concept. In the years since, *hexie* has declined in prominence as this policymaking buzzword has ceased to be a political priority. Today's Chinese IR literature more frequently reflects current President Xi Jinping's emphasis on *renlei mingyun gongtongti*, a concept that is likewise rhetorically linked to traditional Chinese ideas regarding harmony but is perhaps better suited to the intensely globalised present.

DOI: 10.4324/9781003259794-5

If tradition-rich concepts are shorthand for certain visions of world politics, then it is not necessarily historical usage that counts. When used by researchers today, *tianxia*, *guanxi*, and *gongsheng* are statements of intent, not historical user manuals.

Making peace with the Chinese state

China's non-competitive domestic political system has not produced a uniform IR theory. The various strands of present-day IR research are perceived as belonging to different 'schools': *tianxia* and *guanxi* belong to the 'Beijing School', *gongsheng* to the 'Shanghai School', and *daoyi* to the 'Tsinghua School'.[4]

Chinese IR scholarship is nevertheless sensitive to government policy. Chinese universities and other research institutions are deeply embedded within state and party structures. Critical and probing IR scholarship is encouraged and rewarded as long as it is deemed conducive to the flourishing of the nation and compatible with central government policy.

There is a common stereotype in the West that Chinese scholars are simply doing the work of the state. This stereotype inaccurately presents Chinese scholars as a monolithic body that is unable to act creatively and that straightforwardly takes orders from the government. As we have seen, the Chinese IR community has hosted spirited internal debates, has been adept at engaging in new theorisation, and has offered alternatives to current ways of thinking about interactions among polities. It is nevertheless true that government policy influences the scope of political thought within the Chinese IR community. Thus, for example, as different in outlook as the *guanxi* and *daoyi* theories may be, they both play out in the same ideologically bounded space. Furthermore, Chinese scholars may be inclined to turn their attention to issues and problems that the state has identified as particularly worth researching.

One advantage to the integration of research and policymaking networks is that innovative researchers are well placed to influence policy. The theories are in a sense designed to be applicable within the Chinese state as it exists today, and policymakers are aware of this. A disadvantage is that researchers who wish to make a difference must couch their work in terms that respond constructively to existing policy frameworks. The three theoretical approaches considered here are interesting in this regard as they draw inspiration from both longstanding and more recent government policy while also presenting alternative trajectories or expanded ambitions for this policy.

For example, Chinese foreign policy has long championed Westphalian sovereignty.[5] The Chinese IR theories' visions of interdependent polities may be seen as subtly challenging this emphasis. Indeed, traditional Chinese thought has explicitly been used for this purpose in the past.[6] The challenge is not revolutionary; it must be seen in light of a strong Chinese tradition of what Zhang Yongjin terms "discursive engagement with the Westphalian ideal."[7] None of the Chinese IR theories considered here deny the existence or relevance of sovereign states, but neither do any of them regard pursuit of state interests as the immediate priority in harmonious world politics. That is, the theories are all constructed to be complementary with the Chinese policymaking environment while also advocating new approaches to foreign policy.

It is thus important to avoid creating a false binary that sees scholars as either being opposed to the state or as being mere communicators of or apologists for state power.[8]

The risk of exceptionalism and ethnonationalism

Because Chinese IR is understood in both China and the West as distinctly Chinese (for better or for worse), it has largely been applied to thought experiments and situations involving China. *Tianxia* theory is primarily situated in the field of political philosophy and envisions a world politics utopia. *Gongsheng* theory has developed into an approach espousing a particular kind of world political practice aimed at producing symbiotic relations among polities. *Guanxi* theory has an epistemological focus, presenting a Chinese alternative to understanding world politics such as they are, though Qin Yaqing clearly sees the relational approach as especially conducive to peaceful attainment of shared interests.

As we have seen, Chinese IR theories do not always acknowledge the real philosophical differences underlying the various ancient Chinese schools of thought from which they draw. This is itself in keeping with the Chinese tradition of selectively repurposing past intellectual traditions. Chinese IR theorists' use of ancient Chinese thought clearly makes their theories more amenable to contemporary Chinese foreign policy. This does not mean that their use of traditional thought is superficial. To the contrary, all three theories considered here suggest in various ways that harmonious relations are the natural state of the world or that virtuous or successful social actors are those that pursue harmony. In Taoist and Confucian thought, skill and virtue arise out of knowledge, and knowledge is achieved through practice: to act harmoniously is to know the way of heaven. This logic is (intentionally) circular, but it is embedded within Chinese theories of harmonious IR: *tianxia* is achieved by knowing the world as world, *guanxi* is achieved by relating more and more harmoniously, and *gongsheng* is achieved by deepening mutual dependencies.

Qin argues that conflict between polities is the norm in part because political thought is oriented around existential competition between autonomous actors.[9] But what good is it to conceptualise mutually beneficial relations between polities on the basis of ancient Chinese thought when scholars elsewhere are unlikely to pay much heed to Confucius and Mozi? One answer is that this simply does not matter: these are Chinese theories designed for the Chinese public. The theories in question nevertheless seek to engage with and to some extent argue on the terms of mainstream IR. For example, researchers working with all three Chinese theories considered here draw upon game theory to show the benefits of their approaches.[10] Yet success in the world politics 'game' requires a shared understanding of its rules. The harmony-seeking Chinese approaches all attempt to either change the rules of the game as it is now played or to suggest that many international actors have misunderstood the existing rules.

Chinese IR theory simultaneously promotes a world politics of peaceful coexistence and mutual respect *and* describes these values as distinctively Chinese. In one respect, this can be seen as a strategic move: flattery of the Chinese state may be an effective means of gaining influence over policy. There are risks, though, in arguing that the ideal form of world politics comes naturally to China: these theories challenge the West's epistemic privilege but struggle to escape the East-West binary this privilege has produced. As Zhang Feng comments:

> The government and some intellectuals have taken an undifferentiated West as the Other in constructing the uniqueness of the Self, producing a discourse about the West as exploitative and aggressive and China as benevolent and peaceful. This is a process of essentializing both the Western and Chinese traditions through selective use of historical narratives. China's exceptionalism is partly constructed through this key mechanism of essentialization by selection: certain aspects of history and culture are selected to fit exceptionalist narratives, and in the process create myths.[11]

Shifting the "locus of enunciation," in Walter Mignolo's words,[12] would be an enormous achievement for Chinese IR research and practice. It would not, however, necessarily either free China from the conceptual dominance of Western theory or produce theories that are convincing to many people outside China and are thus capable of challenging the universalism of Western theory.

Although Chinese IR theories are primarily designed for Chinese consumption, Chinese IR theorists are themselves aware of the potential for these theories to be either misunderstood or understood unsympathetically in the West. Zhang Feng expresses concern that *daoyi* theory could be "misinterpreted by foreign scholars as advocating a model of post-imperial hierarchical international politics in the service of China's future hegemony."[13] In contrast, harmony-oriented theories with historical undertones may appear less threatening: "The pacifist discourse also has important political and ideological functions. . . . In addition to elevating China to the moral high ground, it is also meant to dissipate the fear and suspicion about a rising China."[14]

It is indeed possible to deploy the *tianxia*, *guanxi*, and *gongsheng* theories to suggest that China's growing role in the world and its enhanced interest in global governance are essentially benign. Yet proclamations of benignity are not universally convincing. The influential public intellectual Xu Jilin proposes a "new *tianxia*-ism" (新天下主义 *xin tianxia zhuyi*) as a remedy to destructive forces of nationalism, including Chinese nationalism:

> Behind the upsurge of nationalism in China today is a value system that emphasises Chinese exceptionalism. It believes that the West has Western values and China has Chinese values; therefore, China should not follow the evil path of the West but its own special path to modernization. This kind of argument, which seems very patriotic and nationalistic, is the least "Chinese" and most anti-traditional, because the Chinese tradition of civilization is not grounded in nationalism but *tianxia*, whose values are universal and humanistic rather than exceptional. . . . After the introduction of nationalism from Europe in modern times, the Chinese people's mind became much narrower and their civilization was diminished. From the grandeur of *tianxia*, where all humans can be integrated into the cosmos, Chinese civilization narrowed to the pettiness of "that is Western, and this is Chinese." Mao Zedong once spoke of "China's need to make a greater contribution to humanity," arguing that "only when the proletariat liberates all of humanity can it finally liberate itself," which reveals a broad vision of internationalism behind his nationalism. But all we find in today's Chinese Dream is the great revival of the Chinese nation.[15]

Xu's presentation of an open-minded, non-hierarchical 'new *tianxia*-ism' is intended as a challenge to what he sees as Chinese IR's implicit exceptionalism: if *tianxia* theory is intended to introduce a higher purpose than that of the state to world politics, then *tianxia* cannot be used to promote the interests of one state above others.

Even this approach is liable to be seen as nationalistic, given that it remains grounded in theories and concepts that originated in China. Discussing *tianxia* theory, Chu Sinan suggests it is logically inconsistent for

Chinese IR scholars to simultaneously seek to counter "epistemic colonialism" and to advocate a theory that some view as "inherently authoritarian and betray[ing] a longing for a Sinocentric order resembling imperial China."[16] Chu lists ten criticisms of *tianxia* theory that have emerged in the literature:

> (1) selective and arbitrary reading of the Chinese philosophy and history, (2) unsubstantiated or exaggerated claim of the Chinese culture's pacifism, (3) uncritically prioritizing the "Chinese experience" in theory building, (4) celebrating hierarchy and authoritarianism, (5) deemphasizing the patriarchal legacy in Confucianism, (6) implicit racism toward ethnic minorities, (7) projection of "racial sovereignty" overseas, (8) rigid adherence to a "West vs. non-West" binary, (9) advocating a Sinocentric world order, and (10) serving as a cover for Chinese nationalism.[17]

All these criticisms of *tianxia* theory have been present in the literature, but some seem misplaced. Zhang Feng argues that today's *tianxia* theory is an attempt to "reinvent the concept of *tianxia* as a way of thinking about world politics," not a longing for imperial China or a desire to recreate the past.[18]

These critiques nevertheless link back to the troublesome issues surrounding epistemic positioning and decolonial scholarship, which we discussed in Chapter 2. It is necessary to interrogate the criticism directly.

In defence of epistemic positioning

Everyone has a perspective. Everyone has a knowledge. Everyone is positioned somewhere on the mountain.[19]

To understand what we are seeing, we must first be aware of our position.

A Chinese classical garden can be seen from many perspectives. It can be seen from a bird's-eye view: all-encompassing, at the centre of everything, but somewhat flat and unconducive to discerning interactions. It can be seen from ground level, at the edge of the lake: cognisant of its partiality but permitting great insight into the observer's situation. It can be seen from above but from a specific position, for example, from atop a pagoda at the south end of the lake: clearly situated within the garden and thus subject to its workings, yet also with a wide view of the city or mountains beyond, depending on where the observer chooses to direct their gaze.

And there are many other possibilities. Regardless, the things we see only make sense if we know where we are located.

The Chinese IR theories we consider here all situate themselves first in China and then, subsequently, somewhere more specific, localised in accordance with their selected mix of ideas and ideals. Like all theories, they each have their limitations. But knowledge of where they are positioned is not among these limitations. Even *tianxia* theory, which insists on seeing the whole world, knows that it is seeing the whole world from China.

As we saw in our discussion concerning claims of epistemic difference, Chinese IR theory has been criticised for being forthright about its status as something specifically Chinese. Such criticism, though often well-meaning, is characteristic of coloniality. The West's epistemic privilege allows it to take its own perspectives as standard: Western intellectual traditions are the invisible backdrop to ostensibly objective mainstream IR theories. Erasure of non-Western perspectives becomes a precondition for being taken seriously as theory, even for theories that are designed to challenge Western epistemic privilege. William A. Callahan, a staunch critic of Chinese IR theory, writes of Zhao's *tianxia*:

> While Zhao understandably criticizes the West for universalizing its particular worldview at the considerable expense of other worldviews, is he doing anything different? Is not he trying to universalize the very particular Chinese concept of Tianxia in order to apply it to the world? And does not Zhao's *Pax Sinica* risk creating the very problems of an intolerant world order that he seeks to solve? Rather than a post-hegemonic world order, does not Tianxia script a new hegemony?[20]

Callahan here accuses *tianxia* theory of being epistemically hegemonic and universalising in intent. The alternative, however, would seem to be a theory that limits its own relevance to Chinese affairs, a theory that does not attempt to challenge Western universalist rhetoric.

In making his argument, Callahan overlooks his own positioning within a particular epistemology. He sees Chinese perspectives as Chinese but takes Western perspectives for granted. His is a knowledge without a knower. In the first paragraph of his article, Callahan writes: "Rather than simply provide suitably Chinese parallels to 'international,' 'security,' or other mainstream IR concepts, many public intellectuals in Greater China have been promoting the ancient concept of '*Tianxia*' to understand Chinese visions of world order."[21] In other words, *tianxia* is problematic because it fails to follow the script written by "mainstream IR concepts" that exist in a cultural vacuum.

Why, we might ask, should Zhao content himself with creating Chinese equivalents to 'international' or 'security' if he evidently believes that the 'international' is subordinate to the 'global' and that 'security' mistakes cause for effect? Why not instead demand that Callahan produce his own IR theory along Chinese lines? Such a request would be not just absurd but also fundamentally wrong—not because particular intellectual traditions should only be open to particular kinds of people[22] but because insistence upon the replacement of self with the other is the worst kind of epistemic violence.

The intention here is not to attack Callahan, many of whose wider arguments have merit. The intention is to show that, notwithstanding China's powerful position in the world today, Chinese IR scholarship is subject to the same pernicious double standards imposed by the 'mainstream' scholarship as are so many other non-Western intellectual traditions. Chinese researchers of world politics are expected to de-position themselves completely, to exist outside the world. Yet they are simultaneously expected to refrain from speaking to the world. They are warned not to particularise but also not to universalise. Like so many Black and Indigenous scholars, they are warned not to be too emotional, too confrontational, or too rooted in their own traditions, yet they are labelled inauthentic or have their fields of recognised expertise circumscribed if they attempt to move beyond the ethnic limitations that have been forced upon them.[23]

The answer to Western epistemic privilege is not for Chinese researchers to chase the phantasm of theory that exists beyond culture, history, context, experience, and knowledge. The Chinese past may yet be of use to the Chinese present, and if that proves disturbing or not worthwhile to some Western scholars, then so be it. For, in fact, most of the Chinese IR theorists are not actually trying to convince people like Callahan; they are trying to convince the public, policymakers, media, and scholars in China.

They do, however, wish to be understood by Western scholars, hence their use of tools such as games theory.

Let us return to our gardens.

The logical response to learning about the existence of divergent traditions of landscape architecture in imperial China and early modern Europe is not to insist that one theory concede its inferiority to the other. Nor is it to insist that both sets of theory be combined until any particularity has been erased. The solution is instead perhaps to acknowledge the legitimacy of both kinds of theory, while retaining the ability to choose which sort of garden one prefers. A European landscape architect who is aware that classical Chinese gardens follow a different logic than do formal European gardens is still entitled to apply European standards of taste when assessing Chinese gardens. If one believes that a certain thing is beautiful and useful, then knowledge that other people like other things is not an argument against one's own beliefs. Such knowledge may, however, affect the manner in which one chooses to approach those who have different beliefs.

The next chapter considers the application of Chinese IR theory to foreign policy practice in order to follow this line of thought: why does it matter whether the public, policymakers, media, and scholars in the West understand the thinking and motivations of Chinese IR theorists?

Notes

1 Wang & Jiang 2019, 130; Sterckx 2019, 209–230.
2 Sterckx 2019, 34.
3 Gao 2019.
4 Zhang et al. 2014; Guo 2017; Lu 2019, 2018; Qin 2019.
5 Zhao 2018.
6 Ling 2013.
7 Zhang 2008, 101.
8 Chu 2020, 22.
9 Qin 2018.
10 Zhao 2009; Guo 2017; Qin 2018; Lu 2018; Yao 2019.
11 Zhang 2013, 317.
12 Mignolo 2002, 938.
13 Zhang 2012.
14 Zhang 2013.
15 Xu 2015.
16 Chu 2020, 2–3.
17 Chu 2020, 4.
18 Zhang 2010, 110.
19 Qin 2018, ix.
20 Callahan 2008, 756.
21 Callahan 2008, 749.
22 Ling 2017.
23 Gegeo 2001.

References

Callahan WA (2008). Chinese visions of world order: Post-hegemonic or a new hegemony? *International Studies Review, 10*(4), 749–761.

Chu S (2020). Whither Chinese IR? The Sinocentric subject and the paradox of Tianxia-ism. *International Theory.* Epub ahead of print.

Gao H (2019). 稷下黄老学与先秦诸子百家—论《管子》对先秦诸子学的整合与扬弃. 社会科学战线, *292*(10), 47–55.

Gegeo DW (2001). Cultural rupture and indigeneity: The challenge of (re)visioning "place" in the Pacific. *The Contemporary Pacific, 13*(2), 491–507.

Guo S (2017). 中国国际关系理论建设中的中国意识成长及中国学派前途. 国际观察, *145*(1), 19–39.

Ling LHM (2017). World politics in colour. *Millennium, 45*(3), 473–491.

Ling LHM (2013). *The Dao of world politics: Towards a post-Westphalian, worldist international relations.* Routledge.

Lu P (2019). 中国特色国际关系理论建设的阶段性进展与不足. 国际关系研究, *40*(4), 74–83.

Lu P (2018). 理解中国国际关系理论的两种构建途径. 世界经济与政治, *449*(1), 73–93.

Mignolo W (2002). The enduring enchantment (or the epistemic privilege of modernity and where to go from here). *The South Atlantic Quarterly, 101*(4), 927–954.

Qin Y (2019). 中国国际关系理论的发展与贡献. 外交评论, *180*(6), 1–10.

Qin Y (2018). *A relational theory of world politics.* Cambridge University Press.

Sterckx R (2019). *Chinese thought: From Confucius to Cook Ding*. Penguin.

Wang Q, & Jiang X (2019). 中国传统和谐观为什么历千年而弥新. 人民论坛, *628*(11), 128–130.

Xu J (2015). 新天下主义与中国的内外秩序. 知识分子论丛, *13*(1), 3–25.

Yao L (2019). 论国际关系中的"共生安全". 国际观察, *157*(1), 51–66.

Zhang C, Yu H, Zhang J, & Zhou S (2014). 海纳百川,包容共生的"上海学派". 国际展望, *33*(6), 1–17.

Zhang F (2013). The rise of Chinese exceptionalism in international relations. *European Journal of International Relations*, *19*(2), 305–328.

Zhang F (2012). 中国国际关系研究中的清华路径. 国际政治科学, *32*(4), 125–156.

Zhang F (2010). The tianxia system: World order in a Chinese utopia. *Global Asia*, *4*(4), 108–112.

Zhang Y (2008). Ambivalent sovereignty: China and re-imagining the Westphalian ideal. In Jacobsen T, Sampford C, & Thakur R (Eds) *Re-envisioning sovereignty: The end of Westphalia?* (101–116). Routledge.

Zhao S (2018). A revisionist stakeholder: China and the post-World War II world order. *Journal of Contemporary China*, *27*(113), 643–658.

Zhao T (2009). *坏世界研究：作为第一哲学的政治哲学*. 人民大学出版社.

6 Applying Chinese IR theory to foreign policy practice

Harmony in the Belt and Road Initiative

Harmony is not a hidden agenda

Chinese IR theory frequently presents Chinese and Western thought as essentialised binaries. However, the world is larger than just 'China' and 'the West'. Within Chinese IR, little attention is granted to theory that is neither Chinese nor Western. The supposition may be that non-Western polities will be more receptive to Chinese approaches simply because they are non-Western. This overlooks the cultural contingency of theory in which many arguments in favour of explicitly Chinese IR theory are grounded. It also risks reinforcing colonial power structures that seek to divide the world into this or that sphere of influence and serve to ignore the agenthood of all except the 'great powers'.[1]

The harmony-oriented Chinese IR theories considered here nevertheless all present visions of world politics that are said to benefit all polities, not just polities of a particular kind (for example, Western liberal democracies or socialist states). Certainly, the Chinese government's outward-oriented rhetoric emphasises making common cause with other states on issues of mutual concern. Chinese leaders regularly highlight the so-called Five Principles of Peaceful Coexistence (和平共处五项原则 *heping gongchu wuxiang yuanze*, hereafter 'Five Principles') as guiding China's foreign policy. The Five Principles, arising from Sino-Indian diplomacy and the Non-Aligned Movement in the early 1950s, consist of mutual respect for sovereignty and territorial integrity, mutual non-aggression, non-interference in one another's internal affairs, equality and mutual benefit, and peaceful coexistence. In the dual context of decolonisation movements and the newly formed People's Republic of China's struggles to gain international recognition, the Chinese government had good reasons for embracing the Five Principles "as the basic norm for international relations" that could overcome "differences in political and social systems."[2]

Continued official commitment to the Five Principles conceals changes in China's foreign policy over the decades. Under the Reform and Opening Up

DOI: 10.4324/9781003259794-6

(改革开放 *gaige kaifang*) policy beginning in the late 1970s and 1980s, Chinese policymakers sought to expand the country's international economic activities and, eventually, international political activities to "discuss and cooperate with all countries in an effort to establish a new international order that is stable, rational, just, and conducive to world peace."[3] Crucial to this has been the *tai ji* (太极) technique of conflict avoidance, which has seen the Chinese state seek to skirt international confrontation.

Tai ji foreign policy has not prevented international actors—often well-meaning and earnest in their assessments—from interpreting Chinese actions as threatening and aggressive, especially with Chinese state and business actors playing increasingly prominent roles internationally. The foreign perception of a threatening and free-riding China has prompted official and scholarly efforts in China to more clearly articulate and theorise the country's foreign policy methods and objectives.[4]

None of the Chinese theories considered here are content with the present international order, which they regard as both biased in the West's favour and likely to produce conflict. All three theories call, in different ways, for a radical deepening of China's relations with other polities and for entering into relations of intense interdependence because they all envision such interdependence as essential for peace and prosperity in world politics. Within *tianxia* theory, failure to deepen dependencies between polities is indicative of a 'failed world'.[5] Within *guanxi* theory, relational (Chinese) approaches foster interdependence and shared production of power, whereas rational (Western) approaches are conducive to anarchy and existential competition.[6] Within *gongsheng* theory, only genuine symbiosis can assure the success of the world's community of common destiny.

Western commentators often accuse China of secretly seeking to make other states dependent upon it. These commentators are wrong about this effort being secretive, but they are correct about the pursuit of dependency. The Chinese IR theories considered here all advocate just such dependency. Furthermore, the policy frameworks that have helped inspire these theories and that these theories have helped inform are not *just* about promoting trade and win-win cooperation. The policy documents and pronouncements produced by the Chinese state in support of these frameworks make clear that they seek harmony, not *mere* coexistence.

The desire for enhanced dependency has only been secretive and hidden in the sense that official Chinese statements have not been understood on Chinese terms. Speaking before the United Nations General Assembly in 2015 about the challenges raised by globalisation, Chinese President Xi Jinping said:

> As an ancient Chinese adage goes, "The greatest ideal is to create a world truly shared by all." . . . All countries are interdependent and

share a common future. . . . Development is meaningful only when it is inclusive and sustainable. To achieve such development requires openness, mutual assistance and win-win cooperation. . . . In their interactions, civilizations must accept their differences. Only through mutual respect, mutual learning and harmonious coexistence can the world maintain its diversity and thrive.[7]

Discussion of shared interests and shared power, symbiosis and interdependence, mutual constitution and common destiny, and harmony as the path to peace, which are so critical to Chinese IR research and foreign policy pronouncements, are simultaneously alien and disruptive to much Western IR discourse. In these particular Chinese visions of world politics, security arises out of harmonious relation. This harmony is infinite and without end, a relational process that can never be completed. Yet such a harmony may be impossible to perceive for those whose epistemological starting point is the 'ontology of existence.'[8] By the same token, balances of powers, opposing alliances, conditions of hegemony or bipolarity, and adjacent or distant spheres of influence may be perceptible only through a lens of competition among individually rational actors. Although efforts have been made to bridge the gap,[9] Western and Chinese IR theories may perceive the same empirical data in fundamentally different ways.

Next, we consider how inattentiveness to Chinese perspectives or lack of understanding of Chinese IR theory can cause misinterpretation of the rhetoric surrounding Chinese foreign policy. We take the case of the Belt and Road Initiative.

A harmonious Belt and Road Initiative?

The Belt and Road Initiative (BRI, formerly One Belt, One Road) is an overarching policy framework focused on creating links between China and other states as well as links among these other states. The BRI was originally envisioned as consisting of an overland Silk Road Economic Belt (a set of connections between China, Central Asia, West Asia, and Europe) and an oceanic 21st-century Maritime Silk Road (MSR) (a set of connections between China, Southeast Asia, South Asia, West Asia, East Africa, and Europe). The project has, over time, grown to encompass all the world's regions, with islands of the Pacific now being included as part of the MSR and with Arctic states and territories being included in a Polar Silk Road or Ice Silk Road.

The BRI is usually seen as having its origins in a pair of speeches by President Xi Jinping in 2013, but the BRI concept was first set forth in detail in a 2015 policy document titled *Vision and Actions on Jointly Building Silk Road Economic Belt and 21st-Century Maritime Silk Road*.[10] This document presents the BRI as an initiative promoting economic prosperity and regional economic cooperation, principles of mutual consultation, joint construction and sharing, policy coordination, and mutually beneficial development.

Although the BRI is widely recognised as both a major area of Chinese policy attention and as having a significant impact on the world, research into the BRI often struggles to define what is being studied.[11] The BRI has been variously described as a geostrategic and geoeconomic programme seeking to advance Chinese interests,[12] a mixed strategic and economic strategy,[13] and a model of inclusive globalisation.[14] Lee Jones and Zeng Jinghan portray the BRI as a flexible and multifaceted framework for political action:

> Projects like BRI are not meticulously planned by top leaders; rather, they are loose "policy envelopes," whose parameters and implementation are shaped by internal struggles for power and resources. They are kept deliberately vague to accommodate these diverse interests, creating wide latitude for them to influence, interpret and even ignore top leaders' wishes.[15]

The BRI's abstract nature means that its impacts, both positive and negative, cannot be assessed or discussed with much accuracy or rigour.[16] This creates serious risk of miscommunication in China's foreign relations.

In international discourse, the BRI is often presented as focused on loans and foreign direct investment by China, in creation of factories, construction of transport infrastructure such as roads and ports, and activity in extractive industries such as mining. Discussions of the topic often fail to differentiate between activity by the Chinese state and activity by Chinese companies (state owned or privately owned). Furthermore, foreign scholars pay relatively little attention to the formal people-to-people exchange, knowledge and technology sharing, research collaboration, and welfare promotion initiatives that are the focus of many Chinese studies on the BRI.

It is nevertheless correct that much of the activity conceived of as within the BRI is directly economic in nature. Western scholarly, popular media, and political settings have given particular attention to the manner in which such Chinese activity may represent 'debt-trap diplomacy'. The notion is that 'China' (as a monolithic state actor) is extending loans that it knows small or developing states will struggle to repay, with the aim of seizing assets or gaining diplomatic leverage once the debtors default. This is a core part of the 'China threat' discourse that presents Chinese overseas activity as threatening the environmental, social, economic, cultural, and military security and sustainability of countries and territories around the world.[17]

Other scholars have countered that the notion of 'debt-trap diplomacy' is not rooted in reality. The polities in question take loans from many states, companies, and institutions; there is little evidence of the Chinese state gaining diplomatic concessions as a result of holding debt; specific instances of 'debt-trap diplomacy' are difficult to identify; and the few, oft-repeated examples (e.g., Chinese military support base in Djibouti, Hambantota Port in Sri Lanka, the attempted leasing of Tulagi, in the Solomon Islands) tend to be based on oversimplified or highly speculative analyses.[18]

Many people in China regard accusations of debt-trap diplomacy as spurious and ill intentioned. However, the idea that the BRI is a tool for debt-trap diplomacy may instead be a matter of biases arising from different perspectives, producing divergent interpretations of the same events.[19]

Given that the provision of loans to small or developing polities is hardly a new phenomenon and has long been pursued by states, companies, and institutions based in the West, why has an anti-China narrative arisen specifically with regard to Chinese lending activity? We suggest that this might relate to China's own conceptualisation and communication of the BRI.

Western states frequently discuss their lending to and investment in small or developing polities in terms of selfless charitable support or promotion of domestic industries, depending on the intended target audience.[20] In contrast, Chinese foreign policy discourse tends to foreground mutual benefit. Chinese government statements position the BRI in terms of creating and strengthening processes of interaction and exchange for the wellbeing of all humankind. Chinese IR theorists commonly regard as a core Chinese cultural attribute the Confucian idea of self-help being rooted in the helping of others. In such a context, the notions of either truly selfless charity or truly self-centred industrial promotion make little sense.

We may illustrate these divergent approaches by comparing two speeches, given on comparable occasions, by Chinese President Xi Jinping and US President Joe Biden, respectively.

In a speech at the Boao Forum for Asia on 20 April 2021, President Xi said:

> Where should humanity go from here? What kind of future should we create for future generations? . . . It is crucial that we bear in mind the shared interests of mankind and make responsible and wise choices . . . The Belt and Road Initiative (BRI) is a public road open to all, not a private path owned by one single party. All interested countries are welcome aboard to take part in the cooperation and share in its benefits. Belt and Road cooperation pursues development, aims at mutual benefits, and conveys a message of hope. . . . "By setting sail together, we could ride the wind, break the waves, and brave the journey of ten

thousand miles." We may at times encounter stormy waves and dangerous rapids, but as long as we pool our efforts and keep to the right direction, the giant vessel of human development will stay on an even keel and sail toward a brighter future.[21]

Such sentiments match well with the harmonious ideals expressed in the three Chinese IR theories we have considered. There is a sense of shared destiny, the need for collaborative effort, and an understanding that cooperation and engagement may be ends in themselves.

Just two days later, on 22 April 2021, President Biden spoke at the virtual Leaders Summit on Climate:

> When people talk about climate, I think jobs. Within our climate response lies an extraordinary engine of job creation and economic opportunity ready to be fired up. That's why I've proposed a huge investment in American infrastructure and American innovation to tap the economic opportunity that climate change presents our workers and our communities . . . All of us, all of us—and particularly those of us who represent the world's largest economies—we have to step up. You know, those that do take action and make bold investments in their people and clean energy future will win the good jobs of tomorrow, and make their economies more resilient and more competitive. . . . And this summit is our first step on the road we'll travel together . . . to set our world on a path to a secure, prosperous, and sustainable future. . . . The countries that take decisive action now to create the industries of the future will be the ones that reap the economic benefits of the clean energy boom that's coming.[22]

Both presidents are calling for global action on issues of global concern. Both even use the metaphor of a shared path or road. However, the two national leaders deploy quite different strategies and make quite different assumptions in their appeals to mixed foreign and domestic audiences. The Chinese argument prioritises shared interest, asserting that success for all is dependent upon care for all; the American argument prioritises self-interest, asserting that pursuit of personal advantage can benefit others too.

Neither argument is more or less altruistic than the other, and neither is more or less capable of success or capable of being deployed for good or for ill. But the premises of the arguments differ. They may result in different ways of expressing political objectives and in different ways of pursuing these objectives. The Chinese argument is premised upon everyone being a winner: win-win cooperation (a modernised, globalised rendering of the traditional concept of mutual care) is at the heart of BRI rhetoric, even if it cannot be guaranteed in practice. The American argument is premised upon interstate competition: although everyone will win if countries work to combat climate change, those that compete best will win most.

Western observers may be more accustomed to President Biden's argument, which justifies helping others by foregrounding self-interest. However, Western observers, for whom the dyad of self-care/other-care might not come naturally, may be suspicious of President Xi's argument, which could appear to be a denial of self-interest. A Western observer might well regard China's self-interest as concealed and wonder what China is trying to get out of the BRI. From a Chinese perspective, though, the self-interest in President Xi's appeal is evident, for it will have been assumed from the start that self-interest is served by collective action and support for others.

Some observers in both China and the US may suspect that such lofty proclamations by world leaders often amount to little more than hollow statements of intent, that leaders are trying to impress, placate, or propagandise through rhetoric. It is nevertheless significant that these Chinese and US appeals are only truly effective in their own cultural contexts. The fact that China and the US struggle to actually achieve the promise of these political visions does not render them empty or meaningless. These statements each speak to their respective audiences; the Chinese discourse of harmony and US discourse of competition possess limited cross-cultural appeal.

The BRI is in many senses amorphous and abstract. It is difficult to say where the BRI begins and ends. Tellingly, many of the projects associated with the BRI—including controversial projects like Hambantota Port—predate conceptualisation of the BRI. Thus, scholars and policymakers alike frequently ask: what can be done to ensure that the BRI is greater than the sum of its parts? Yet this may be the wrong question.

The constituent 'parts' of the BRI may not be the totality of projects that fall or are drawn under its umbrella. Within a harmony-oriented theoretical framework, the BRI may instead be understood as a method of seeing and foregrounding harmonious interaction. The next sections provide examples of how Chinese scholars in the social sciences have used theories of harmonious IR to make sense of the BRI and, just as significantly, to argue that the BRI should take certain directions.

A *tianxia* perspective on the BRI

From the perspective of *tianxia* theory, the BRI could be seen as a nascent system for governing beyond the state. Indeed, the official discourse surrounding the BRI leans heavily on the idea that one can succeed only if all succeed, leading to a Mohist ideal of impartial mutual care. The world is already composed of interdependent polities; the BRI is just a method of creating recognition of this interdependence and prompting people to act accordingly.

The *tianxia* perspective is frequently reflected in Chinese scholarship. Qian Kun asserts that the BRI's promotion of win-win cooperation and aid to developing countries, such as infrastructure construction, can be seen as a step toward establishing a harmonious *tianxia* system.[23] Li Chunlin, Chen Jianqing, and Adam Grydehøj conceptualise the BRI "as a framework for global governance with the potential to provide global public goods," representing "a vision of the world in which the success of one country can only be guaranteed by the success of all. The BRI is only a success if all its member states develop and prosper in tandem."[24]

Teng Wensheng links the BRI and the building of a community of common destiny with *tianxia*, regarding them as sharing the same essential spirit: "Whether it is to promote a new type of international cooperation, improve global governance, establish a more just and equitable international political and economic order, or realize a new economic globalization," the BRI and the notion of community of common destiny all serve to achieve *tianxia* ideals.[25] Bao Jianyun similarly argues that the BRI represents China's "strategic vision of being a major country that can achieve the *tianxia* ideals."[26]

Men Honghua asserts the essentially Chinese nature of *tianxia* while at the same time suggesting that *tianxia* is good for the world. This is in contrast with the post–World War II Marshall Plan of the US, which Men sees as fostering conflict:

> The BRI, reshaping the relationship between China and the world, is the strategic starting point and core path for China to realize its ideal of *tianxia*. A comparison between China's BRI and the United States' Marshall Plan shows fundamental differences in China's and the United States' paths of realizing their ideals of the world. The BRI is based on shared development and the principle of equality and mutual benefit, guided by pragmatic cooperation and aiming at joint discussion, co-construction and shared benefits, while the other was essentially a political and security strategy, in which the United States started the Cold War process with the Soviet Union through conditional aid.[27]

Zhao Tingyang's own writings show more interest in explicating the concept of *tianxia* than in distinguishing it from specifically Western thought. However, explicit comparison between Chinese *tianxia* ideals and Western perspectives, such as that engaged in by Men Honghua, is common in the wider literature. For example, Luo Shengrong and Lan Li note that "domestic research on the BRI focuses on such factors as rule of law, intercommunication, and governance, while foreign academic circles focus on soft power outputs."[28] These differences in focus reflect a more essential conflict between the ideal of great harmony under heaven and the Western-centric worldview. Because of this, Luo and Lan argue, China must "strengthen its awareness of international discursive power, formulate its international political communications strategy, and promote the international community's understanding and awareness of China's aim of building a community of common destiny."[29] That is, the BRI's success depends upon people elsewhere in the world understanding the meaning of China's *tianxia* ideals, despite their different epistemic starting points.

Bao Guangjiang and Yang Peixin argue that the BRI promotes a distinctively non-Western commitment to *tianxia*. There is an ongoing "shift from an initial pursuit of individual, family, group, and national interests to today's increasing attention to the overall interests of the world," highlighting "the limitations of Western values":

> First, the mainstream values of today's international society have a strongly Western nature and are insufficiently inclusive of non-Western civilizations, global care, and pluralistic values. Second, the international system and order established under the dominance of Western values cannot solve shared global problems. Third, it is difficult for Western values to truly conform to the future developmental direction of the international community. It is here that the BRI is so significant. The rise of shared problems is a major feature of today's international society. . . . Western countries with the core concept of "sovereign nation-centricism" firmly believe in instrumental rationality, which often causes the international community to fall into the dilemma of the individual rationality of the state and collective irrationality of the world.[30]

Bao and Yang's vision is rooted in *tianxia* theory, but their language recalls that used by Qin Yaqing to argue his *guanxi* approach. This highlights how Chinese scholars outside the IR discipline itself often adopt the various lines of Chinese IR theory in part and in tandem. The theories are mixed and matched in a way that resembles the theorists' own use of diverse strands of ancient Chinese thought. This is also the case in the Western social sciences, in which non-IR researchers will not always be aware of the theoretical demarcations that define the IR discipline.

A *guanxi* perspective on the BRI

From the perspective of *guanxi* theory, the BRI's goal is to encourage relations between polities. The BRI should be assessed in terms of these relations. The BRI's various channels and programmes for promoting inter-action between polities serve to develop trust and intimacy. This renders instrumental rationality inappropriate and is conducive to the construction of relations of mutual benefit. The closer the relationship between actors, the more dependent they become on one another, and the more they all ben-efit. This disincentivises actors from breaking off relations; to do so would both sacrifice the benefits arising from the relationship and cause unmet needs for actors that had previously been dependent upon one another.

Whereas *tianxia* is a vision of the real world as an ideal world, *guanxi* theory is situated ambiguously between a description of how relationships between social actors work and advocacy for a particular kind of foreign relations practice. As such, even though *guanxi* theory has had considerable influence outside the discipline of IR, the theory's presence in non-IR writ-ing is often more observable in the use of a particular style of argumentation than it is in deployment of a particular foreign policy strategy.

Asserting the "open and inclusive" nature of the BRI, Huang Fengzhi and Wei Yongyan argue that the BRI's approach to globalisation will disrupt the Western-centric logic of globalisation as well as the centre-periphery power structures that have hitherto dominated international communication and movements of people.[31] Chen Weiguang and Wang Yan argue:

> A new governance model for the BRI should be developed, one that draws upon the traditional relations-based governance of the East and rules-based governance of the West. Relations are conducive to the for-mation of consensus between China and the countries along the Belt and Road and the shaping of the cognitive basis for building a community of common destiny, while rules provide an institutional basis for the BRI's infrastructure construction as well as trade and investment facilitation, etc. Within the BRI, relations-based governance and rules-based gover-nance can play alternative and complementary functions, depending on different participants, different stages, and different issues.[32]

Yang Siling connects the concept of *guanxi* with traditional Chinese thought, suggesting that *guanxi* drives China's approach to the BRI and has "important ideological significance in constructing state-to-state relations." Yang argues, "Only by attending to relations-based governance can China and the countries along the Belt and Road establish a commonly accepted paradigm and set of rules in the interactive process of international relations as well as strengthen cooperation for the common good."[33]

Yu Xiaofeng and Zhang Taiqi agree with Qin Yaqing that Western IR the-ories, focusing on the system level, neglect the dimension of sociality, espe-cially the dimension of *guanxi xing* (关系性 relationality). They maintain that the BRI, based on peace and cooperation, is a kind of multidirectional co-construction and form of cooperative companionship as well as a system of reciprocal *guanxi zhuyi* (关系主义 relationalism) and harmonious linkage.[34]

Using Qin Yaqing's *guanxi* theory as their analytical framework, Xie Baoxia, Zhu Xianlong, and Adam Grydehøj present the BRI as "an uncentred network of relation" encompassing polities that each bring their own interests, histories, and perspectives (sometimes shared, sometimes not) into relation. Contrasting this relational approach with ideas of essentialised East-West conflict, they argue that it may be "more productive to perceive a vast, mutually constituted archipelago than to perceive a system of centre-periphery tensions and binary conflict."[35] That is, from a *guanxi* perspective, the BRI can be a means of overcoming strict divisions and assumptions of conflict between China and the West.

A *gongsheng* perspective on the BRI

From the perspective of *gongsheng* theory, the BRI can promote shared peace and prosperity by guiding polities toward relations of symbiosis or mutual dependence. Whereas *tianxia* theory sees all polities as already mutually dependent, and *guanxi* theory sees all social actors as constituted through interaction with specific other actors, *gongsheng* theory is focused on encouraging interdependence. The world represents a community of common destiny, but the long-term shared prospects for humankind are poorly served when individual polities have divergent short-term and medium-term interests. The symbiosis sought by *gongsheng* theory involves coordinating and aligning the interests of polities so that they must be addressed collectively.

Zhang Qianxiao and Li Jialin apply *gongsheng* theory to their analysis of industrial transfer between China and BRI countries. They argue that the BRI presents a "historic opportunity for industrial transformation, upgrading, and economic development. It has further strengthened international cooperation and division of labor, interlinked value activities among countries and regions, and deepened the 'symbiotic relationship' between them."[36] Similarly, Liu Xuelian and Shen Na maintain that "The BRI has built a platform for equal participation and shared development of developing countries . . . in a *gongsheng* system."[37] Yi Baozhong and Zhang Jieyan recall *gongsheng* theory's origins in the natural sciences when they suggest that "the theory of symbiosis, which describes the extended material connections between one or more members of different species in population ecology, is highly adaptable to solve the cooperative problem of the BRI construction in Northeast Asia."[38]

Xia Liping proposes the term 'symbiosis system theory' (共生系统理论 *gongsheng xitong lilun*) as a combination of *gongsheng* theory and systems theory. Xia believes that symbiosis system theory can "play an important role in establishing One Belt, One Road." He argues that China should use symbiosis system theory to guide BRI policymaking and should promote the BRI as a form of systems engineering, with the aim of establishing a symbiotic international system.[39]

Gongsheng theory has also lent itself to studies of more specific aspects of the BRI. For example, Li Hongying applies symbiosis system theory to universities within the BRI, perceiving higher education as "a symbiotic mechanism for economic, cultural, scientific, and technological development along the route."[40] Discussing *gongsheng* theory in terms of industrial transfer to BRI countries and bilateral value chain upgrading, Liu Youjin, Yin Yanzhao, and Zeng Xiaoming argue that "mutual benefits and symbiosis are important foundations for sustainable implementation of the BRI."[41] Yao Lu and Jing Jing use the *gongsheng* approach to argue for the urgency of conscious movement toward symbiosis in response to the Covid-19 pandemic: a global governance model must be created to effectively address shared challenges for the good of the world as a whole and to facilitate the emergence of a positive community of common destiny.[42]

Yu Xiaozhong and Luo Xia apply *gongsheng* theory to energy cooperation in the BRI: "Due to the complexity and systematic nature of energy cooperation along the Belt and Road, it must be studied from a deeper perspective of symbiosis." Taking *gongsheng* theory as their analytical framework, they use adaptability analysis to study symbiotic units related to energy policy, facilities, and funds as well as to study the win-win but unequal, random, and unstable characteristics of symbiosis. They propose four strategic trajectories (stabilising units, consolidating foundations, optimising the environment, and improving interfaces) to promote symbiotic energy cooperation within the BRI.[43]

Prioritising harmony over power

Although Chinese IR theories are frequently accused of boosterism and ethnocentricism, the previous examples suggest the need for a more nuanced understanding of their use in the wider scholarship. When these theories are applied to the BRI, it is seldom as a means of arguing that China is an ideal international actor. The theories are instead used more narrowly to assert the centrality of principles of harmony within the BRI. One effect of this is that the BRI's (and by extension, the state's) aims of widened and deepened interconnectivity receive theoretical justification. Ideals of mutual benefit are foregrounded in the process and are presented as crucial to the BRI's success.

Proclamations of the BRI's potential for constructing a community of common destiny may be read as boosterism, exceptionalism, or ethnonationalism by many Western scholars. Far from being mere cheerleading of government policy, scholarly applications of harmony-oriented IR theory often seem to be efforts at keeping China honest, attempts at encouraging Chinese state and private actors to abide by their own rhetorical, cultural, or political ideals. When scholars argue that Chinese tradition prioritises harmonious relations over coercive power, it is not a method of saying that China is better than everyone else; it is a technique for inspiring better policy and holding decision makers to account. It is a technique that allows Chinese policy and practice to be (often implicitly) criticised without being seen to challenge state or party legitimacy. The theories have thus proven useful as tools for connecting particular theoretical ideals with the realms of policy and practice. Policy frameworks such as the BRI and theories of harmonious relation in world politics are mutually productive and interdependent.

All three of the harmony-oriented Chinese IR theories considered here regard shared interests among polities as inherent, and all three regard mutual dependencies as either pre-existing or worth cultivating. Mutual dependence is a condition that should be embraced or enhanced, not regretted or avoided. The BRI is designed to increase positive interactions of all kinds between polities. These include relations of mutual economic dependence.

No relationship between social actors is based on absolute equality. It is obvious that many countries will become more dependent on China than China is on them. From the perspective of the theories considered here, though, the pursuit of strong relationships is valuable in itself. The BRI is more than just a collection of bilateral relationships between China and other states precisely because the BRI imagines a community of mutually dependent social actors. In such a community, China might be the single most powerful actor without necessarily dominating the whole. Qin, for his part, argues that power is always shared because power arises out of social relations. He writes, "Once a relationship is established, power is no longer absolutely private."[44] That is, even if China is the dominant partner in a relationship, its power is not a characteristic of self but is instead tied to the relationship. This is conducive to the maintenance of mutually beneficial relationships among polities.

From the perspectives of these Chinese IR theories, dependence as such is not problematic. This contrasts with what Qin terms "egoistic rationality based upon the ontology of the isolated self-existence" in Western thought, including IR.[45] Such an ontology tends to denigrate dependence and elevate independence, producing the ideal of a polity that can make all its own decisions in pursuit of absolute self-interest.[46] While the *tianxia* ideal of universal dependence and impartial mutual care might be difficult to imagine in practice (such is our difficulty in seeing the world as world), so too is the ideal of absolute independence in a world in which all polities—from the most weak and isolated to the most powerful and central—depend on relations with others to achieve their goals.

We thus suggest that Western suspicions concerning the BRI may partially be a result of differing approaches to the world in general and to world politics in particular. A Chinese discourse that sounds suspiciously selfless to Western observers may not be perceived in this manner by Chinese IR theorists and policymakers. Equally, whereas dependent (even mutually dependent) relations run counter to much Western thinking regarding sovereignty and statehood,[47] the exercise of relations and arrangement of parts into harmonious order has become a shared priority within Chinese IR theory.

This does not guarantee that China's international activities will be beneficial to all polities. It is entirely possible that the BRI will jeopardise certain Western privileges. Furthermore, it is inevitable that the BRI will include projects that serve some interests better than others. Harmonious rhetoric will not always be matched by realities on the ground.

We do not argue here that the BRI is necessarily the best or the only option for solving global problems. We simply suggest that the ways in which the BRI is perceived are influenced by underlying, culturally contingent ideas about how world politics works (both in practice and as an ideal) as well as by the dynamics of China's closely intermeshed scholarly-policymaking network.

Notes

1 Davis, Munger, & Legacy 2020; Grydehøj et al. 2021.
2 Jia 2019, 730.
3 Chen 1993, 243–244.
4 Zhang 2013, 306.
5 Zhao 2009a.
6 Qin 2018, 265.
7 Xi 2015.
8 Qin 2018, 121–123.
9 Shih 2020, 2019.
10 National Development and Reform Commission, Ministry of Foreign Affairs, & Ministry of Commerce 2015.
11 Stec 2018.
12 Cai 2017.

13 Flint & Zhu 2019.
14 Liu & Dunford 2016.
15 Jones & Zeng 2019.
16 Grydehøj et al. 2020.
17 Grydehøj et al. 2021.
18 Brautigam 2020; He 2020; Wallis 2020.
19 Brautigam 2020, 6–7.
20 Kapoor 2008.
21 Xi 2021.
22 Biden 2021.
23 Qian 2020, 149.
24 Li, Chen, & Grydehøj 2020.
25 Teng, 2019, 10.
26 Bao 2019, 112.
27 Men 2020, 50.
28 Luo & Lan 2020, 13.
29 Luo & Lan 2020, 22.
30 Bao & Yang 2019, 138–139.
31 Huang & Wei 2019, 70–73.
32 Chen & Wang 2016, 93.
33 Yang 2015, 15–16.
34 Yu & Zhang, 2015, 9–10.
35 Xie, Zhu, & Grydehøj 2020.
36 Zhang & Li 2021, 125.
37 Liu & Shen 2021, 6.
38 Yi & Zhang 2015, 65.
39 Xia 2015, 30.
40 Li 2018, 23.
41 Liu, Yin, & Zeng 2020, 136.
42 Yao & Jing 2021.
43 Yu & Luo 2021.
44 Qin 2018, 242.
45 Qin 2018, 139.
46 Grydehøj 2020.
47 Alberti & Goujon 2020.

References

Alberti F, & Goujon M (2020). A composite index of formal sovereignty for small islands and coastal territories. *Island Studies Journal*, *15*(1), 3–24.

Bao G, & Yang P (2019). 身家国天下: "一带一路"合作中的四层价值体系. *东南学术*, *271*(3), 130–139.

Bao J (2019). 基于"一带一路"倡议的习近平国际战略观. *马克思主义研究*, *228*(6), 110–119.

Biden J (2021, April 22). Remarks by President Biden at the virtual Leaders Summit on Climate opening session. *White House*. www.whitehouse.gov/briefing-room/speeches-remarks/2021/04/22/remarks-by-president-biden-at-the-virtual-leaders-summit-on-climate-opening-session/

Brautigam D (2020). A critical look at Chinese "debt-trap diplomacy": The rise of a meme. *Area Development and Policy*, 5(1), 1–14.

Cai P (2017). *Understanding China's Belt and Road Initiative*. Lowy Institute.

Chen Q (1993). New approaches in China's foreign policy: The post-Cold War era. *Asian Survey*, 33(3), 237–251.

Chen W, & Wang Y (2016). 共建"一带一路": 基于关系治理与规则治理的分析框架. 世界经济与政治, 430(6), 93–112.

Davis S, Munger LA, & Legacy HJ (2020). Someone else's chain, someone else's road: US military strategy, China's Belt and Road Initiative, and island agency in the Pacific. *Island Studies Journal*, 15(2), 13–36.

Flint C, & Zhu C (2019). The geopolitics of connectivity, cooperation, and hegemonic competition: The Belt and Road Initiative. *Geoforum*, 99, 95–101.

Grydehøj A (2020). Unravelling economic dependence and independence in relation to island sovereignty: The case of Kalaallit Nunaat (Greenland). *Island Studies Journal*, 15(1), 89–113.

Grydehøj A, Bevacqua ML, Chibana M, Nadarajah Y, Simonsen A, Su P, Wright R, & Davis S (2021). Practicing decolonial political geography: Island perspectives on neocolonialism and the China threat discourse. *Political Geography*, 85, 102330.

Grydehøj A, Davis S, Guo R, & Zhang H (2020). Silk Road Archipelagos: Islands in the Belt and Road Initiative. *Island Studies Journal*, 15(2), 3–12.

He A (2020). The Belt and Road Initiative: Motivations, financing, expansion and challenges of Xi's ever-expanding strategy. *Journal of Infrastructure, Policy and Development*, 4(1), 139–169.

Huang F, & Wei Y (2019). "一带一路"倡议与建设对传统地缘政治学的超越. 吉林大学社会科学学报, 59(2), 66–73.

Jia G (2019). New China and international law: Practice and contribution in 70 years. *Chinese Journal of International Law*, 18(4), 727–750.

Jones L, & Zeng J (2019). Understanding China's "Belt and Road Initiative": Beyond "grand strategy" to a state transformation analysis. *Third World Quarterly*, 40(8), 1415–1439.

Kapoor I (2008). *The postcolonial politics of development*. Routledge.

Li C, Chen J, & Grydehøj A (2020). Island climate change adaptation and global public goods within the Belt and Road Initiative. *Island Studies Journal*, 15(2), 173–192.

Li H (2018). "一带一路"倡议与区域高等教育合作的共生机制及推进策略. 现代教育管理, 342(9), 23–28.

Liu W, & Dunford M (2016). Inclusive globalization: Unpacking China's Belt and Road Initiative. *Area Development and Policy*, 1(3), 323–340.

Liu X, & Shen N (2021). 丝绸之路经济带建设对中国周边关系的多层次建构. 哈尔滨工业大学学报(社会科学版), 23(2), 1–8.

Liu Y, Yin Y, & Zeng X (2020). 中国向"一带一路"国家产业转移的互惠共生效应—基于双边价值链升级视角的研究. 经济地理, 40(10), 136–146.

Luo S, & Lan L (2020). 国内外学界对人类命运共同体研究的比较及启示. 世界民族, 142(6), 13–25.

Men H (2020). 中国的世界理想及其实现维度. 世界经济与政治, 476(4), 27–52.

National Development and Reform Commission, Ministry of Foreign Affairs, & Ministry of Commerce (2015). *Vision and actions on jointly building Silk Road Economic Belt and 21st-century Maritime Silk Road*. Ministry of Foreign Affairs of the People's Republic of China.

Qian K (2020). 全球化时代的"天下"观、"大国叙事"与"命运共同体"—王斑、钱坤教授访谈. 首都师范大学学报(社会科学版), *256*(5), 142–150.

Qin Y (2018). *A relational theory of world politics*. Cambridge University Press.

Shih CY (2020). Re-worlding China: Notorious tianxia, critical relationality. *E-International Relations*. www.e-ir.info/2020/09/02/re-worlding-china-notorious-tianxia-critical-relationality/

Shih CY (2019). *China and international theory: The balance of relationships*. Routledge.

Stec G (2018, February). China's Belt and Road Initiative is neither a strategy, nor a vision: It is a process. *European Institute for Asian Studies*.

Teng W (2019). 丝绸之路的历史与人类命运共同体. 国际汉学, *21*(4), 5–17.

Wallis J (2020). How should Australia respond to China's increased presence in the Pacific Islands? *Security Challenges*, *16*(3), 47–52.

Xi J (2021, April 20). Full text: Keynote speech by Chinese President Xi Jinping at the opening ceremony of the Boao Forum for Asia Annual Conference 2021. *Xinhua*. http://en.people.cn/n3/2021/0420/c90000-9841049.html

Xi J (2015). Working together to forge a new partnership of win-win cooperation and create a community of shared future for mankind (New York, 28 September 2015). *Embassy of the People's Republic of China in the Republic of Fiji*. http://fj.china-embassy.org/eng/topic/xjpjh/t1321127.htm

Xia L (2015). 论共生系统理论视阈下的"一带一路"建设. 同济大学学报(社会科学版), *26*(2), 30–40.

Xie B, Zhu X, & Grydehøj A (2020). Perceiving the Silk Road Archipelago: Archipelagic relations within the ancient and 21st-century Maritime Silk Road. *Island Studies Journal*, *15*(2), 55–72.

Yang S (2015). "一带一路"倡议下中国与沿线国家关系治理及挑战. 南亚研究, *112*(2), 15–34.

Yao L, & Jing J (2021). 以共享促共生：疫情冲击下全球治理转型的中国推进. 东北亚论坛, *30*(2), 113–126.

Yi B, & Zhang J (2015). 东北亚地区"一带一路"合作共生系统研究. 东北亚论坛, *24*(3), 65–74.

Yu X, & Luo X (2021). "一带一路"能源共生合作：框架分析与推进路径. 甘肃社会科学, *251*(2), 198–206.

Yu X, & Zhang T (2015). "和合主义"：建构"国家间认同"的价值范式—以"一带一路"沿线国家为例. 西北师大学报(社会科学版), *52*(6), 5–12.

Zhang F (2013). The rise of Chinese exceptionalism in international relations. *European Journal of International Relations*, *19*(2), 305–328.

Zhang Q, & Li J (2021). 新时期优化产业转移演化路径与构建双循环新发展格局—基于共建"一带一路"背景下产业共生视角的分析. 西北大学学报(哲学社会科学版), *51*(1), 124–136.

Zhao T (2009a). A political world philosophy in terms of all-under-heaven (Tianxia). *Diogenes*, *56*(1), 5–18.

7   Conclusion

This book has explored the role of harmony in Chinese IR theory. We have found that harmony is a key—if contested—concept in a number of influential strands of Chinese IR theory, which approach harmony, world politics, and the world itself in different ways. The *tianxia*, *guanxi*, and *gongsheng* theories all argue that practicing world politics in different and more harmonious ways can create better results for the world as a whole.

What is harmony? In *tianxia* theory, harmony is produced through knowledge: *tianxia* is seeing the world from above, seeing the world as world and acting accordingly, for the good of the world. In *guanxi* theory, harmonious relations arise out of understanding that power, identity, and interests are always shared with particular others. In *gongsheng* theory, global problems call for the conscious construction of a community of common destiny: once symbiosis has been achieved, major conflict is unthinkable, and shared interests will be prioritised. In keeping with the explicitly relational nature of these theories, harmony is simultaneously process and result, means and end.

Although the theories share a focus on harmonious relations, they conceive of these relations in different ways and suggest different methods of achieving them. At its most basic level, shorn of theory-specific characteristics, harmony can perhaps be defined as *avoidance of conflict through pursuit of shared interests*.

The theories and theorists do not exist in isolation. All are reflected, refracted, and reinforce a continually evolving field of Chinese IR scholarship and foreign policy practice. This is partly because Chinese IR theory and foreign policy inform one another: scholars create theories that are amenable to China's policymaking environment, and policymakers use these theories to guide and innovate policy, which in turn affects the kinds of research scholars perform.

None of these theories are proponents of China's foreign policy *status quo*. They all seek to move Chinese foreign policy in directions that, they

DOI: 10.4324/9781003259794-7

argue, are more in line with Chinese tradition. This rootedness in Chinese tradition is not, however, the rationale for the theories. Chinese tradition forms the backdrop of the theories or perhaps their epistemic basis. The theories do not argue that Chinese foreign policy should take a certain direction because it is Chinese, though they do argue that Chinese tradition can assist in perceiving world politics more productively. A great advantage to couching one's theory in ancient concepts such as harmony is that their historical flexibility and ambiguity allows them to be deployed to various ends while also clearly signalling compatibility with the Chinese cultural and policymaking system. A disadvantage is that this exposes the theories to criticism related to the historical use of these concepts, which may be beside the point when a concept is in fact being reinvented for a new era.

Harmony has not been a major area of interest in Western IR scholarship. As we have seen, there is a perception within parts of the Chinese IR community that epistemic individualism and rationality are incapable of perceiving harmonious relations. Yet if harmony can be understood as avoidance of conflict through pursuit of shared interests, then it does not seem so distinct from the world politics ideals of Western IR theory. Where there may be an essential difference is in the emphasis placed on relational rather than autonomous actors. Even when the aims of Chinese and Western IR theory and foreign policy are similar, they seem to understand world politics actors in different ways and thereby engage in different rhetorics of self-interest/other-interest and self-care/other-care.

Chinese IR theorists may have varying degrees of understanding of Western perspectives on world politics, but they know that Western perspectives exist. After all, the Western mindset remains the universal standard within international academia. Efforts to create explicitly Chinese IR theories not only demonstrate a desire to articulate alternative theories grounded in Chinese epistemology but also demonstrate respect for the theoretical legitimacy of Western theory. The Chinese IR theories we consider here may argue that Chinese approaches can potentially produce better outcomes for the world, but they do not argue that Western approaches fail as genuine theory or are not applicable in their own contexts. That is, the Chinese IR theorists and the Chinese policymaking community begin their work with recognition of an epistemic divide.

Mainstream IR is apt to respond by asserting that epistemic divides simply do not exist. Such claims are deeply entangled in coloniality. The West—believing itself to be the world—is blind to its own existence. It encompasses the non-West (a category of its own creation) while insisting on the universality of Western logics and values.

Where do we go from here? This book does not envision a future of global consensus and agreement. That lies beyond us. And if this should someday to come to pass, it is unlikely that the sea change will come from IR scholarship.

But we might hope for a future of better communication and mutual understanding. This requires acknowledging difference—not as essentialised, inescapable binaries but as taking seriously individuals', communities', and nations' ideas of self, encompassing all internal contestations and regardless of whether one agrees with what they entail. While we can wish for a world in which theories developed out of divergent cultural contexts can inspire and build upon one another, the first step is simply understanding. Agreement and accord are secondary to and conditional upon respect and understanding.

One person's 'wolf warrior foreign policy' and 'debt trap diplomacy' may be another person's pursuit of a 'harmonious world' and 'community of common destiny'. The same objectives and activities can be justified and interpreted in different ways.

This is not to say that one perception is right, and the other is wrong. It is not to say that everyone must assess the results of policies on the epistemic bases of those who devise them or carry them out. There are no normative solutions to epistemic divides precisely because such divides are not problems in need of solutions. It is the height of epistemic privilege to accept the legitimacy only of that perspective which happens to be one's own. If not everyone is playing the game of world politics by the same rules, it may be because some people disagree about what kind of game humanity ought to be playing. Adherence to a different set of rules is not necessarily a sign that an actor is acting in bad faith.

It is perfectly possible for someone to understand Chinese intentions behind, for example, the Belt and Road Initiative and still be legitimately opposed to it. Understanding that other people think differently does not preclude holding one's own opinions.

What is needed is neither for Chinese researchers to promote Chinese IR theories as universally applicable to all cultures nor for Chinese researchers to entrench essentialised East-West dichotomies. What is needed is both acknowledgement that perspectives on world politics are culturally contingent and recognition that different perspectives have the right to coexist. It is worse than pointless for epistemologies to engage in existential competition.

What is needed within global IR research is a renewed commitment to respect for difference.

What is needed is harmony.

Index